Today's youth are in desperate need to underst   ll
as to be "ready to give a defense for the hope that is in them" to a lost and hurting
world. Young people have bought the lie that truth is not attainable. With help from
inspirational veterans of ministry to children and their families, *Give Me Jesus* offers
practical training to help us communicate that the gospel is truth and it alone brings
redemption and salvation. With so much in ministry vying for our time and attention,
we need to dedicate ourselves to what really matters and will endure for eternity. This
book deliberately re-focuses our attention toward that important end.

Michelle Anthony
Family Ministry Architect, David C Cook

Every leader should be involved in sharing the life-altering message of the gospel with
all generations—especially children. This book is a practical tool that every leader
should utilize to the max. It will spark your creativity and boost your proficiency in
using a variety of methods to communicate the unchanging gospel.

Frank Damazio
Lead Pastor, City Bible Church
Author, *The Making of a Leader, Strategic Church, Life-Changing Leadership and Strategic Vision*

Ryan Frank has quickly become one of the leading voices and experts in children's
ministry. Now, he has put together some of the brightest minds to create a manifesto
for where ministry to kids is headed. This book will challenge your heart, as well as
your mind. Ryan and his team have nailed it with *Give Me Jesus*.

Brian Dollar
Kids Pastor, First Assembly, North Little Rock, Arkansas
Founder, High Voltage Kids Ministry Resources, www.highvoltage-kids.com
Author, *I Blew It!*, and blogger at www.briandollar.com

I just finished reading *Give Me Jesus*. I opened it two hours before a ministry dinner and
literally excused myself early from the dinner so that I could finish the book. As is evident throughout the text, Ryan Frank's pillars of a gospel-conscious ministry establish
a balanced approach to the evangelism of children. Each writer expertly builds upon
those pillars, providing the children's worker with the motivation and proven practices
to establish a ministry that not only appeals to children's emotion and senses, but also
transforms their hearts. This book has inspired and convicted me. I wish I could sit with,
talk to and pray with every contributing author. The discussion questions at the conclusion of each chapter are brilliant. Every children's ministry leader should read and discuss
each chapter with his or her key leaders and helpers—the results *will* affect the lives of kids
in their churches. My children's ministry students will be required to read *Give Me Jesus*.

Dick Gruber
Professor of Children's Ministry, Valley Forge Christian College

In *Give Me Jesus*, Ryan has pulled together some of my favorite voices in children's ministry. Listen and receive fresh motivation! More than the benefit children's pastors will receive from reading, though, I'm excited that this book can be a tool to put into the hands of every volunteer, driving home the message that they are doing life-changing Kingdom work. The turnover is great among volunteers in children's ministry, and I believe part of that is due to a lack of understanding of how important these workers are in communicating the gospel. They need to know why they're doing what they're doing! They each need to digest *Give Me Jesus*! When you believe the gospel is the center of all you do, there is a desperation and commitment that accompanies the assignment to teach kids. Ryan ends the book with a declaration that Roger Fields wrote years ago. Repeat it every morning as a reminder of your all-out commitment to reach kids with the message of the gospel. It will give you the start you need!

Tina Houser
Executive Editor, *KidzMatter Magazine*
Senior Publications Director, KidzMatter

Ryan Frank brings excellence to all areas of ministry and has assembled some very creative minds to teach us how to help develop gospel-conscious children.

Ron Hunter Jr.
D6 Conference Director
Executive Director & CEO, Randall House

If you are a leader and want the ingredients to build an impactful children's ministry centered on the life-changing gospel of Jesus Christ, I would highly recommend this book. Ryan has done an amazing job of speaking into and assembling some of the most passionate leaders in children's ministry who will show you how to develop a heart-transforming kids ministry with Jesus at the center. The greatest legacy is not what we leave *for* people, but what we leave *in* people. This book gives leaders the tools to teach Jesus to kids in a tangible way that will impact the lives of future generations.

Craig Johnson
Director of Ministries, Lakewood Church

In order for children to grow up to become the leaders God designed them to be, they must first be introduced to the God who designed them! Teaching the gospel is the most fundamental aspect of children's ministry, yet for the most part, it is often done ineffectively. By reading this book, you will you discover tools that will make sharing the gospel with children a strength of your ministry, not a weakness. Trust me, this is a manual that belongs on every children's pastor *and* senior pastor's shelf, and its pages should be well worn from use.

Mike Johnson
Director of Childhood Leadership Development, Fellowship Church
Executive Producer, LeadershipForKids.tv

In an age when we hear from multiple people at multiple times on multiple days it's refreshing to hear a perspective on the value of *One*. Once you get beyond this church or that church, mega church or other church, my opinion and your opinion, *one* thing remains: the gospel of Jesus. Ryan reminds us that our methods are many but our vision is *One*.

Craig Jutila
President, Empowered Living, Inc.
Author *Hectic to Healthy* and *Faith and the Modern Family*
www.whowillyouempower.com

In children's ministry we have the privilege of showing kids Jesus for the first time. This privilege is a joy, but it is also a weighty responsibility. There are many things we can teach our kids each week, but if we could hear the cry of every child's heart, I think it would be what Ryan and his friends are pleading with you to do: just give them Jesus, because Jesus is everything!

Sam Luce
Campus Pastor, Redeemer Church in Utica, New York
Blogger at www.samluce.com

In recent years I've noticed that Ryan has been talking about something that very few KidMin leaders seem to be talking about: keeping the gospel central in our children's ministries. This is an equipping and inspiring resource that you'll want to share with all of your key leaders.

Matt Markins
Executive Director of Ministry Resources and Vice President of Marketing and Strategy, Awana

As a senior pastor for over 20 years, a lecturer of management at the Naval Postgraduate School and founder of KidLead Inc., I'm convinced that the most critical focus of the Church should be on kids. This book should be read by children's ministry workers, senior pastors and parents. While I like pretty much everything Ryan Frank creates, I especially appreciate this book because it brings together expert views on the most important topic next to Jesus Himself: helping kids follow Him.

Alan E. Nelson, Ed.D.
Founder, www.kidlead.com

Give Me Jesus reflects the heartbeat of a solid children's ministry—the gospel. This well-written book will challenge you to examine your ministry through the writings of many experienced children's ministry leaders who are passionate about teaching kids the Word of God. As you apply these practical ideas, your ministry will become more dynamic and focused on winning souls for Christ.

Kris Smoll
Director of Discovery Land (Children's Ministries)
Appleton Alliance Church, Appleton, Wisconsin

Wow! This book is really needed for today's children's ministries. We hear about young adults who were raised in the church, some having graduated from Christian colleges, yet they turn their backs on the Lord. We ask ourselves: *Why?* If this book were front and center in every children's Sunday school, many more would come to know Christ in a deeper way and their lives would be saved from destruction. Wow again! Look at all the experts who have contributed to this book. Chapter by chapter you will encounter one experienced children's worker after another offering insight and inspiration. This book is necessary for children's ministry.

Elmer Towns
Dean Emeritus, School of Religion and Theological Seminary at Liberty University

Give Me JESUS

Give Me JESUS

Gospel-Centered
Children's Ministry That
Changes Lives

GENERAL EDITOR

RYAN FRANK

BETHANYHOUSE

a division of Baker Publishing Group
Minneapolis, Minnesota

Contents

Foreword by Jack Eggar 11

Introduction 13

PART 1: What Is a Gospel-Centered Ministry?

1. Pillars of a Gospel-Conscious Ministry...................................19
   Ryan Frank

2. Why Children Are the Most Important People in the Church................33
   Damon DeLillo

3. Threads: Weaving Jesus into the Lives of the Next Generation................43
   Donna Lucas

PART 2: How to Build Your Ministry on the Gospel

4. The Seven Factors in a Gospel-Centered Ministry 61
   Steve Adams

5. Too Little for the Gospel?..77
   Jenny Funderburke

6. A Ready Defense..93
   Ken Ham

7. Special Needs 111
   Marie Kuck

8. Partnering with the Youth Ministry.. 123
   Chad Miller

9. The Gospel in a Digital Age 133
   Matt McKee

PART 3: Who Shares the Gospel with Children?

10. How to Effectively Share the Gospel with Children 149
    John and Crystal McLennan

11. Training Volunteers to Share the Gospel with Confidence 165
    Jim Wideman

12. Mom, Dad and Salvation 181
    Larry Fowler

PART 4: What Do You Want the Outcomes to Be?

13. Discipleship Cookbook: What a Discipled Kid Looks Like 201
    Roger Fields

14. Equipping Children to Be Missional 213
    Beth Guckenberger

Epilogue 227
    Ryan Frank

Foreword

IT'S ALL ABOUT JESUS

Have you ever said a word over and over until you forget what it means? Like "spaghetti." Or consider a word that is so common and used so often in your field of work that after a while, you lose touch with its meaning. Such is the case with the word "gospel." It's a word commonly used in the ministry, and just like saying "spaghetti" over and over and over, it can lose its true meaning. It's time to define it (or be reminded of its meaning) and focus our ministries on it.

We live in a time when too many curricula, churches and children's ministries have lost their focus—a focus on the gospel. Instead of proclaiming the gospel and all its truth, there are many who opt for what will attract and keep families. Now, there is nothing wrong with using technology, music and other popular elements in children's ministry. These can be very effective tools, but they, along with everything else in ministry, need to be gospel-focused. Too often we downplay the lifesaving truth in order to accomplish other goals. But placing the gospel message at the center of everything, and keeping it simple, is the master key that unlocks the door to a successful, fruit-bearing children's ministry.

Ryan Frank reminds us in a practical way to keep the gospel simple—and to keep its message at the core of our ministries. Using seven pillars and the knowledge of veteran children's ministry leaders, he shows us how to create a gospel-conscious ministry.

I think we all agree that the good news of the gospel can be understood by a child and yet it requires a lifetime to fully plumb the theological depths of John 3:16 alone. That's why it's essential to not only build our ministries on the gospel, but to train those leaders and teachers under our direction how to share it confidently with children. So many of them know the basics, but they often struggle with how to convey them to a child.

Just like a chef would not make an elaborate and intricate recipe without an understanding of the final result, we shouldn't attempt to make disciples without understanding, truly understanding, what a disciple is, what a disciple looks like and the characteristics that a disciple displays.

Children are important to God, children are important to you, and children are important to their parents. And it is during the young, formative years, that families and the church have the opportunity and responsibility to present the truth of the gospel to children. It's possible that these precious ones will be in your shoes one day—grown-up (more or less!), working in ministry and burdened with a desire to reach the children in their ministry. What do you want them to recall from their childhood? What do you want them to know and understand at a young age that you didn't?

Ryan's love for God and His littlest children is contagious, inspiring and absolutely genuine. So read on and allow Ryan and others guide and encourage you as you seek to place the gospel at the core of your ministry; then you too will be as convinced as I am that children can, should and need to grow up to know, love and serve Jesus Christ.

Jack Eggar
President and CEO of Awana

Introduction

"Will you teach Junior Church for a few weeks until we find someone else?" Sound familiar? That was the question that started my venture in children's ministry. I was 17 years old and loved my church. (I still do today.) I was willing to do whatever the church needed—especially "short-term" commitments like this. Well, guess what? They never found anyone else.

Those were special days. Our Junior Church met in a corner of the church gym. Every Saturday, we set up chairs, a PVC pipe puppet stage and our AV equipment (which pretty much was composed of a guitar amp and an overhead projector that would overheat if left on too long). I had a good teacher back in those early days. His name was Pastor John Slater. He mentored me and taught me the basics of children's ministry. He taught me two important things back then: (1) how to visualize my lessons, and (2) how to give away great "quiet seat" prizes! Those two things will make a big difference!

About a year after saying I would teach for "a few weeks," I was invited to attend a series of classes taught by our local Child Evangelism Fellowship missionary. In that series of classes, the importance of effectively evangelizing children was communicated. I was introduced to the Wordless Book, a tool that I still use today. Do you know what the Wordless Book is? It's a book without words. (I'll bet you would have never guessed.) Each page is a color, and each color helps you explain the gospel to kids.

By the way, I've spent time studying the origin of the Wordless Book. The farthest back I can trace it is with the great nineteenth-century evangelist Charles Spurgeon. History records that he used a piece of black paper, red paper and white paper to share God's plan for salvation, back in 1866, at the Metropolitan Tabernacle in London. The black page reminded him of his sin; the red represented Christ's blood shed for him; and the white page stood for the cleansing of his sins through Christ's work on the cross. In 1875, his contemporary D. L. Moody used the Wordless Book in Liverpool, England. He added a gold page to represent heaven.

The Wordless Book made it easy for me to share the gospel with kids. It was a tool that connected with kids and helped them understand God's great love for them. By God's grace, I've seen many children come to know the Lord through the use of the Wordless Book. Of course, we know that the power is not in the Wordless Book itself. The power is in the message—the gospel of Jesus Christ.

That is what this book is all about—the power of the gospel. In fact, Paul said it well when he wrote, "For I am not ashamed of the gospel, for it is the power of God for salvation to everyone who believes" (Rom. 1:16, *ESV*).

You may not know this (but if you do, pretend that you don't), but Alfred Nobel, the founder of the Nobel Peace Prize, was also the guy who created dynamite. When he came up with this new technology, it created a big bang. (Insert laugh here.) He knew he needed a name for his new creation. He had a friend who knew the Greek language, and he asked his friend what the Greek word for "explosion" was. That word was *dunamis*; and so Nobel named his invention "dynamite."

Now go back with me to Romans 1:16, *ESV*: "For I am not ashamed of the gospel, for it is the power of God for salvation to everyone who believes." The word "power" in this verse is translated from that same Greek word: *dunamis*.

So think of dynamite; think of something dynamic; think the fourth of July; think of a giant explosion, and you will have an idea of what Paul was saying. There is explosive power in the simple message of the life, death and resurrection of Jesus Christ. The gospel is powerful.

If I were a gambling man (which I'm not), I'd bet that you already know that. You have experienced the power of the gospel in your own life. You believe in the power of the gospel. You have even invested in the gospel ministry. So, why a book on the gospel? Because it is critically important—especially when we are talking about children!

Children are important to God. I have always loved the story of Jonah and the big, ginormous fish. You know the story. Jonah is called to preach to the Ninevites. Instead of obeying, he runs and boards a ship going the other way. God sends a storm to get Jonah's attention. Jonah volunteers to get thrown overboard (in other words, to end his life), but God has other plans. Jonah gets swallowed by the big fish, sits inside of it for three days and lives to tell about it. (Boy, you talk about a testimony!) God gives Jonah another chance, and this time he obeys. He preaches to the wicked people of Ninevah, and they respond to his preaching. They repent! We know the end of the story. Instead of being glad, Jonah gets ticked. He begs God to take his life, and he throws a big ol' fit.

I love the very last verse in the book of Jonah. You can find it in Jonah 4:11. After Jonah's temper tantrum, God asks Jonah, "And should I not have concern for the great city of Nineveh, in which there are more than a hundred and twenty thousand people who cannot tell their right hand from their left?" In other words, God says, "Jonah. Didn't you see all of those little kids running through town? I love them! They are worth saving!"

Praise the Lord that kids are important to God. The gospel is for everyone, including kids. In fact, it could be argued that the gospel is a gospel for children! Jesus once said this: "Truly I say to you, unless you turn and become like little children, you will never enter the kingdom of heaven" (Matt. 18:3).

Children are important to you. This book was created because, not only are kids important to God, but they are also important to you. Chances are, if you are reading this book, you have a vested interest in kids. If you are a children's and family ministry leader, you will find this book both affirming and challenging, because you will be encouraged to keep the gospel at the core of everything you do with kids. What we do in the church with kids is more than provide childcare and programs. (That was a great spot for an "Amen.") We are shepherds—spiritual influencers in the lives of children. And the gospel is in the center of it all.

Children are important to the church. The church is just one generation from extinction, if you stop and think about it. Just one. The church shouldn't have a passive attitude toward children's ministry. It's quite the opposite. The church needs to make a fresh, aggressive commitment to take children's ministry seriously and keep the gospel the center of everything it does.

I don't want you to hear from just me. When I first talked to Regal Publishing about this book idea, I let them know that I wanted to include several other voices in the book. You're going to hear from several of my friends, who are actively involved in children's ministry and who I deeply respect. On top of that, they each have something very important to say about the gospel as it connects to sweet spots in their ministries. You're going to read different topics, by different writers, each with a different emphasis—but on one theme: the gospel.

I trust that you will appreciate our approach to this book. You're going to get some great teaching and content preassembled with handles! We want the content to be so practical that you can't wait to start making things happen. We have also ended each chapter with discussion questions. These are great for personal reflection or for a group learning activity.

Now, let's dig in. What does it look like to have a gospel-conscious children's ministry? Great question. I'm glad you asked. Chapter 1, here we come.

—Ryan Frank

PART 1:

What Is a Gospel-Centered Ministry?

1

Pillars of a Gospel-Conscious Ministry

Ryan Frank serves as vice president of Innovative Strategies at Awana and is the CEO of KidzMatter. Ryan served as a children's pastor for 15 years and still serves in children's ministry every week. He is the author of *9 Things They Didn't Teach Me in College About Children's Ministry,* and he has contributed to several other published works. Ryan and his wife, Beth, live in Converse, Indiana, with their three daughters.

Personal website: www.ryanfrank.com
Blog: www.justfranktalk.com
Facebook: https://www.facebook.com/ryanfrank1975
Twitter: @ryanfrank75
YouTube: http://www.youtube.com/user/JustFrankTalk
Instagram: ryanfrank75
Pinterest: http://pinterest.com/ryanfrank75

Reports keep coming in from all over the globe that confirm it as true. To say that the world is in a state of shock this morning would understate the situation. The event seems to have taken place at the same time all over the world, just about 25 minutes ago. Suddenly, and without warning, literally thousands, perhaps millions, of people just disappeared. Few eyewitness accounts of these disappearances have been clear, but one thing is certain: Millions who were living on this earth last night are not here this morning.

That was the opening scene from the 1972 movie *A Thief in the Night*. In this film, the viewers meet Patty Jo Myers, "a young woman who considers herself a Christian because she occasionally reads her Bible and goes to church regularly. She refuses to believe the warnings of her friends and family that she will go through the Great Tribulation if she does not accept Jesus. One morning, she awakens to find that her husband and millions of others have suddenly disappeared. Gradually, Patty realizes that the Rapture . . . has happened and she and everyone else left behind are entering into the Great Tribulation, the last days of Earth, dominated by the Antichrist."[1]

My dad, who was 18 at the time, sat through this movie not once, but twice, each time resisting the conviction of the Spirit in his life to come to Christ. About a month after that second viewing, he humbled himself and gave his life to Christ. His life was changed by the power of the gospel.

One of the first things my dad chose to do as a follower of Christ was get his family involved in a church that preached the gospel and told people how to be saved. That was my first experience at Liberty Baptist Church, the church I still call home 30-plus years later.

When I was five years old, I was into Spider Man and Matchbox cars. My dad was a car salesman, and I followed in his footsteps, selling Matchbox cars on our living room floor to Spider Man and all of his amazing duos.

I don't remember much about that summer. But I'll never forget Vacation Bible School. I was sitting on the wood pew listening to the Bible lesson. When an invitation was given for the kids to ask Jesus into their hearts, I bounced out of that pew and headed to the front. I remember that walk to this day. I remember where I was sitting. I remember walking forward. I remember going to one of the rooms in the back and praying. I still have the tract that was used to lead me to the Lord. I also remember running out of that room and telling my parents that I had asked Jesus into my heart—at the young age of five.

On the opposite end of life we read about a man we know as Nicodemus (see John 3). You remember him. He was a member of the Sanhedrin. (He had some serious religious credentials.) You know the story. He came to Jesus by night. I've always envisioned him sneaking through town, head covered, dodging the streetlights and people. He asked Jesus how to receive eternal life, and Jesus told him that he needed to be born again. While the Scripture doesn't record his response that night, we see Nicodemus later in the Bible, identifying himself with Jesus (see John 19:38).

This is the power of the gospel. It is simple enough for a child, yet profound enough for a scholar like Nicodemus. The gospel is no respecter of age. It is a message for children. Literally.

According to George Barna, author, speaker and founder of the Barna Research Group, the probability of someone responding positively to the gospel is 34 percent for children between the ages of 5 and 13. That number takes a nosedive to 4 percent for teenagers between the ages of 14 and 18. It creeps up to 6 percent for adults 19 years and older.[2] Stop for a moment and think about those numbers.

In other words, if you presented the gospel to a group of 100 children, statistics tell us that 32 of them would respond positively and choose to follow Christ. If you presented the same gospel message to a group of 100 14- to 18-year-olds, only 4 of them would respond positively. And if you presented the gospel to 100 adults, only 6 of them would respond positively.

This research led Barna to write an entire book to convince pastors that children should be the church's number-one priority. (The book *Raising Spiritual Champions: Why Children Should Be Your Church's Number One Priority* is a few years old, but every pastor should read it.)

The gospel is a message for children. Not only do a majority of people who follow Christ do so when they are children, but also Jesus Himself said (to a group of grown-ups) that unless you *become* like a child, you cannot enter His kingdom (see Luke 18:16-17). God is looking for childlike faith.

I know I'm preaching to the choir, but let this be a fresh reminder that there is power in the gospel. It is powerful enough to reach the heart of a child and to penetrate the intellect of a scholar.

What Is the Gospel?

Do you remember the first time you heard the gospel? There is not a sweeter story than the story of Jesus Christ. The best definition I know for what is the gospel is the "good news" of Jesus Christ.

The gospel is the central theme of the Bible. It's the heartbeat of every book. And it can be summed up like this:

> For God so loved the world, that he gave his only begotten Son, that whosoever believeth in him should not perish, but have everlasting life. For God sent not his Son into the world to condemn the world; but that the world through him might be saved (John 3:16-17, *KJV*).

What an amazing thing that God loves this world! He loves people so much that Jesus, part of the Godhead, left heaven and came to earth in human form. All God, yet all man. He who knew no sin became sin for us. He lived a sinless life and suffered a cruel death.

The late pastor and author A. W. Tozer said this:

> Jesus Christ came not to condemn you but to save you, knowing your name, knowing all about you, knowing your weight right now, knowing your age, knowing what you do, knowing where you live, knowing what you ate for supper and what you will eat for breakfast, where you will sleep tonight, how much your clothing cost, who your parents were. He knows you individually as though there were not another person in the entire world. He died for you as certainly as if you had been the only lost one. He knows the worst about you and is the One who loves you the most.
>
> If you are out of the fold and away from God, put your name in the words of John 3:16 and say, "Lord, it is I. I'm the cause and reason why Thou didst on earth come to die." That kind of positive, personal faith and a personal Redeemer is what saves you. If you will just rush in there, you do not have to know all the theology and all the right words. You can say, "I am the one He came to die for." Write it down in your heart and say, "Jesus, this is me—Thee and me," as though there were no others. Have that kind of personalized belief in a personal Lord and Savior.[3]

If you are reading this book, there's a good chance that you have embraced Christ and the message of the gospel. With the rest of this chapter, I want to talk about what a gospel-conscious ministry looks like. Let's start by telling you what I mean by that phrase.

A gospel-conscious ministry is a ministry that intentionally keeps the gospel at the center of all it does.

In 2 Samuel 6, we read the account of David bringing the Ark of God back to Jerusalem. It's a beautiful story. (Well, all accept for the part of Uzzah being struck dead for touching the Ark on the way to Jerusalem. That's not exactly beautiful.) Once the Ark made it to Jerusalem, there was music, singing and even dancing. The "Baptist" in me always smiles at that part. Why is it that we don't think dancing is strange when a baseball player rounds the bases after the game-winning home run? We don't think it's strange when the winning touchdown is scored or when our own child scores a goal. We think nothing at hands raised at a concert or a touchdown. Why should we get uncomfortable with them when we worship our awesome God? (I'll now step off the soapbox.)

Back to the story. Why did David go to the work of bringing the Ark of God back to Jerusalem? Here's why: He wanted God to be at the center of Israel's daily life. You could say that David wanted the children of Israel to have a God-consciousness.

What's that mean? We know what it means to be cop-conscious. You see a cop, you do what? You slow down. In fact, you not only spot them driving toward you down the road, but you go as far as to look in every potential hiding spot! When you are gospel-conscious, your point of view is the gospel. When you are gospel-conscious, seven truths impact every part of your ministry:

1. The Word of God becomes alive and real.
2. The message becomes more important than the methods.
3. Personal ministry is a calling, not slot-filling.
4. Programming becomes intentional.
5. Children and youth are valued.
6. Parents become allies.
7. The entire world becomes a mission field.

Let's look at these truths a little closer.

The Seven Pillars of a Gospel-Conscious Ministry

When a ministry focuses on the gospel and is intentional about being gospel-conscious, seven principles will always undergird the ministry. You could say they are pillars of a gospel-conscious ministry.

Pillar 1: The Word of God Becomes Alive and Real

What's the point of children's ministry? Why do we do what we do every weekend and Wednesday night? You know how I hope you will answer that question, don't you? The point is not baby-sitting and childcare. It's much greater than that. (Insert a hearty "Amen" here.)

Sometimes we look for new, innovative, creative, dynamic, critical ways to get great results in ministry, all the while overlooking the obvious. As you saw in the introduction to the book, the power is in the gospel of Jesus Christ.

The gospel is found in God's Word. In a gospel-conscious ministry, the Word of God becomes alive and real. By the way, if we tell the kids that the Bible is a powerful, life-changing book, we should present it that way, shouldn't we? (Maybe that can be my next book.)

Don't miss this point: For the Word of God to become alive and real in your and my ministry, it must be alive and real in the life of the teacher. The gospel has the power to daily transform the life of the Christian. Starting today. Starting with you and me.

Pillar 2: The Message Becomes More Important Than the Methods

Methods and programs change. Think of how children's ministry has changed in the last 20 years alone. While methods and programs change, the message never changes! In fact, in a gospel-conscious ministry, the message becomes more important than the methods!

The apostle Paul understood this. He wrote:

> Though I am free and belong to no one, I have made myself a slave to everyone, to win as many as possible. To the Jews I became like a Jew, to win the Jews. To those under the law I became like one under the law (though I myself am not under the law), so as to win those under the law. To those not having the law I became like

one not having the law (though I am not free from God's law but am under Christ's law), so as to win those not having the law. To the weak I became weak, to win the weak. I have become all things to all people so that by all possible means I might save some. I do all this for the sake of the gospel, that I may share in its blessings (1 Cor. 9:19-23).

When I read this passage, I see a Paul who was willing to bag the methods for the sake of the message. When he was with the Jews, he acted like a Jew. When he was around the Gentiles, he acted like a Gentile. Why? To effectively communicate the gospel.

Don't get too attached to methods. The message always trumps method.

Pillar 3: Personal Ministry Is a Calling, Not Slot-Filling

When you have a gospel-conscious children's ministry, personal ministry becomes a calling. After all, you are involved in the most important work in the world—the ministry of the gospel!

Do the workers in your ministry view themselves as volunteers, or servants? Did you know that the word "servant," in one form or another, is used more than 1,000 times in the Bible? I personally counted every one. (Not really.) That means it's a big deal to God and should be to us as well!

When Paul introduced himself in his New Testament letters, he would start with his name and then describe himself as a servant. For example, "Paul, a servant of Christ Jesus" (Rom. 1:1).

What's the difference between a volunteer and a servant?

- A volunteer picks and chooses when and where and who he/she will serve.
- A servant serves despite the cost.
- A volunteer serves when it's convenient.
- A servant serves out of commitment.
- A volunteer fills a slot on the calendar.
- A servant is all in.

When a children's ministry is gospel-conscious, the workers bag the slot-filling mentality and realize they are called to serve in something much bigger than themselves.

If someone were to come and visit your church, what would they see? Would they see a team of sincere servants who are working to connect kids to Jesus and equip them to be growing and faithful followers? Or would they see a group of volunteers who are filling slots on a calendar?

Pillar 4: Programming Becomes Intentional

Speaking of calendars, it's easy to fill the church calendar with this and that. Most churches don't have a problem finding things to put on the calendar. The question is: Are we putting the right items on the calendar?

The more gospel-conscious a ministry becomes, the more intentional those who are serving will be with their calendar and ministry programs. A good example of this is something my good friend Craig Johnson started doing at his church. Craig is the Senior Director of Ministries at Lakewood Church, that small church in Houston. Here is his story:

> After my son was diagnosed on the middle of the spectrum with autism, I began to read the startling statistics centered around kids with special needs. As the family pastor of my church, I had no idea there were so many families who had special needs and so few churches that had anything for them. If the average church in America is 75–100 people, I would guesstimate less than 1 percent of churches have any type of special needs program; yet there are well over 20 million kids and teens with special needs in America alone.
>
> Our church had one room with some caring individuals but nothing that was developing those children like we were our typical kids. One day, as I was walking through our children's area, God spoke to me very intentionally when He said, "Craig, when you look into the eyes of children with special needs, you are looking into My eyes. Those kids deserve the best, just like any other child."
>
> In that moment, God got my attention, not only for our church but to help other churches establish their own special needs ministry. We didn't want to just baby-sit these amazing children; we wanted to develop them and help encourage their parents in the purpose God had for them. We felt a holistic approach (mind, body, soul and spirit) would be an effective way to develop them in our classrooms. The approach led us to develop four stations: the spiritual station

with curriculum; the sensory station; the physical therapy station; and the educational station model. The kids would rotate with their groups based on needs and age, with teacher-student ratios based on the needs of the child.

When news spread in the community and through our church about what was being offered through the Champions Club, families started coming from all over the community. One dad said, "I have not volunteered or been able to sit in a service for years until now. This ministry helped change our lives." Many times these families feel forgotten, rejected in society and left out of the church. Now, God has been gracious to not only help our church but also to come alongside other churches who desire to be intentional in remembering the ones God never forgets.

Pillar 5: Children and Youth Are Valued

When a ministry is gospel-conscious, children and youth are valued. Children are not viewed as a nuisance. They aren't put in the back to be taken care of while the adults do the important stuff. Instead, they become a priority, starting with the pastor and church leadership, and working its way all the way down.

Nine times out of ten, you spot it as soon as you step in the door. One great example of this is Appleton Alliance Church in Appleton, Wisconsin. I first heard about this church about 10 years ago when someone told me it had relocated to a major highway and chose to show their community that children and youth are an important part of their church. I'll let Kris Smoll, children's ministry director, tell the story:

It has always been the heart and passion of Discovery Land to challenge kids to know God, grow in their faith and go out and make a difference in this world for Jesus Christ. Before we built our new facility, we used hallways, baby pools and other creative stations in our small, traditionally styled church to introduce the lessons to kids. Watching the love for the interactive and hands-on portion of the lesson, we knew this needed to be a focus in our new building. Questions such as, "How do we make learning the Word of God fun, memorable and challenging?" drove our design and discussions as we dreamed big before we presented our plans to the architects. We looked at kids of the past, the present and the future to create classical but very creative hands-on learning stations that included a 25-foot-square sand pit that is 3 feet deep, a water station with a waterfall, Legos in custom-designed wooden sailboats, a chalk wall, a box-stacking station, art carts, a giant mission tree house, a Play-Doh station, and more. Everything in our kid-themed building has purpose for educating kids to know, grow and go out into this world to share the good news of Jesus.

God placed Appleton Alliance Church strategically next to a major highway in Appleton, Wisconsin, where people from the community can look into our building through giant windows that face the high-way. Lights illuminate our Bible-themed murals and learning stations, which has caused the community to feel welcome and curious about what is being taught in our building. As families walk through our building, they see fun, but they also see into classrooms that are de-signed for 25 students per class. In these classrooms, dedicated teachers "bring the Bible to life."

Leadership at Appleton Alliance believes in and has supported investing in children because they know that God's Word challenges us to value souls, no matter the age. Each week, stories are shared of families from our community who have attended church because their kids wanted to come to Discovery Land. God is at work as we hear continuous testimonies of kids discovering a true relationship with God and living out their faith. Kids boldly invite their friends and are eager to make a difference in this world. The building is a tool that God is using to make a difference for eternity.

Pillar 6: Parents Become Allies

God's plan for evangelism and discipleship has always started with the home. We see this all the way back in Deuteronomy 6. This is a critically important part of being a gospel-conscious ministry. In fact, an entire chapter of this book is devoted to this very topic.

Although God's plan is for parents to be the primary spiritual leaders at home, a good percentage of Christian parents don't get it. Some literally don't get it—they need to be taught this. Others get it but don't know where to start. Others get it, know where to start, but lack the discipline and commitment needed to make it happen. Reggie Joiner says that most parents fall into one of these four categories:

1. Acquainted
2. Connected
3. Engaged
4. Invested

In a gospel-conscious ministry, we shoot for number 4. We want to help parents get invested in the spiritual lives of their kids. We do that by teaching them and equipping them to sit in the driver's seat spiritually in their home.

Pillar 7: The Entire World Becomes a Mission Field

Finally, when a children's ministry focuses on the gospel, the entire world becomes a mission field. Not only do we see people all around us who need to hear the gospel, but also we do everything we can to help kids be missional in their day-to-day lives.

There are lots of churches out there that get this. They work hard at helping kids think outside of their own world, and they challenge kids to be outwardly focused. One example of this kind of church is Woodmen Valley Chapel in Colorado Springs, Colorado. Here is what their children's pastor, Kevin Gosselin, had to say:

> At Woodmen Valley Chapel, our desire is that the children who come through our program would develop a heart for missions and the world. We strive to help our kids think outside of themselves by providing them with service opportunities, by making them aware of needs in our community, and by using their offerings to sponsor four Compassion International children.
>
> During VBS last June, we partnered with Compassion International to raise money for the Water for Life program. Woodmen's Global Ministries department offered to match what the kids raised, up to $5,000. We were amazed when our kids—kindergarten through fifth grade—brought in close to $8,000! It was exciting to see their hearts expand for people in need in other parts of the world.
>
> I choked up as our kids presented a check for nearly $13,000 to then president of Compassion International, Wes Stafford, during the Sunday

service following VBS. They had raised enough money to provide 236 filtration systems; each system would provide a lifetime supply of clean water to one or more families, directly affecting approximately 14,500 people.

In addition to providing service and giving opportunities to our children throughout the year, we also focus on developing a missional heart in our older kids through a volunteer program called GOOY-WATS (Going Out Of Your Way Always To Serve). Through this program, our fifth- and sixth-graders serve alongside ministry partners in the classrooms of younger children. We hope this opportunity will give them a lifelong passion for service.

Right now, we are exploring the possibility of a family mission trip to Peru this fall, and Kenya next year, to allow our kids to serve God and others in another country along with their families. We hope opportunities like this will allow our children to experience firsthand what God is doing around the world.

What can your church do to help kids see the world around them through God's eyes? Learn from other churches like Woodman Valley, and begin today!

As I wrap up this chapter, let me encourage you with this thought: *Don't feel overwhelmed.* Your mind is probably spinning with ideas and thoughts. This will continue to happen the more you get into the book. Here's what you need to start: Make the decision to have a God-conscious ministry. Say, "Lord, I'm in." If you have already made that commitment, go ahead and make it again. Decide that starting today, you are going to do everything possible to have a gospel-centered ministry. Once you have made that decision, follow these simple steps.

First, begin small. Don't try to change everything overnight. Start small. Tackle one hill and then move to the next.

Second, communicate your decision to have a gospel-centered ministry to your volunteers. (I should call them servants, shouldn't I?) As a leader, it's your job to communicate the vision to the people. Don't expect them to pick it up by osmosis.

Third, pray and ask for God's blessing. I have a hunch that if you choose to be gospel-centered in your ministry and ask God to bless it, He will. Don't you? How could He say no?

Finally, prepare for God's blessing to come pouring in. It might even be more than you think you can handle, so get ready!

DISCUSSION QUESTIONS

1. What is your salvation story? If you are in a group, share around the room.
2. If children's ministry is more than baby-sitting and childcare, how well are we doing in communicating that to our church? What could we do better?
3. If we tell kids that the Bible is a powerful, life-changing book, we should present it that way. What does that mean to you?
4. How has children's ministry changed over the past 20 years? What has *not* changed during that time?
5. Do you agree that message always trumps method? Why or why not?
6. If someone were to come and visit our church, would they see a team of sincere servants who are working to connect kids to Jesus and equip them to be growing and faithful followers? Or would they see a group of volunteers who are filling slots on a calendar? How can we do better to create a servant culture in our ministry?
7. What can we do to be more intentional about programming in our ministry?
8. How well are we doing to communicate to our church and community that children and youth are valued at our church?
9. What are we doing to help parents get invested, on a regular basis, in the spiritual life of their kids? How can we do better?
10. Are the children in our ministry inward-focused or outward-focused?

Notes
1. "A Thief in the Night," film, Wikipedia. http://en.wikipedia.org/wiki/A_Thief_in_the_Night_%28film%29 (accessed September 2013).
2. George Barna, *Transforming Children into Spiritual Champions: Why Children Should Be Your Church's #1 Priority* (Ventura, CA: Regal Books, 2003), p. 33.
3. A. W. Tozer, *And He Dwelt Among Us: Teachings from the Gospel of John* (Ventura, CA: Regal Books, 2009), pp. 136-137.

2

Why Children Are the Most Important People in the Church

DAMON DELILLO

Damon DeLillo is starting a new adventure as the family pastor at Real Life Church in Valencia, California. Before that he was the creative director at Gospel Light while serving as the family ministry pastor at Mission Church in Ventura, California. He has been working with kids and teenagers, producing events, teaching and creating environments for ministry for what seems like 20 years, but is probably more like since 1993. In 2008, he led a church planting team with North Point Ministries. He figures that all the stuff in this bio really doesn't mean a whole lot, but that his relationship with God does. He and his talented and creative wife, Janna, live in Oxnard, California, and are presently enjoying the challenge of raising their five children: Emilie, Corey, Tucker, Gracie and Macie. He can be found blogging at damondelillo.com or on Twitter @cuchoolin.

Back in the day, there was a famous preacher story that circulated amongst what were then known as "Christian Education Directors"—now our Next Generation Pastors. It was told that D. L. Moody had come back from a tent revival meeting where he reported that 2 1/2 people were saved. Whoever he was talking to replied, "You mean, two adults and one child?" D. L. Moody responded, "No, two children and one adult. *When you save a child, you save a life—a whole life.*"

I came to know Jesus when I was six years old, at Vacation Bible School. Over the years, I've found out that I'm not alone. I'm just one of the many people who decided to follow Jesus when they were children, and one of the many people who came to know Christ during a Vacation Bible School week. *Nearly 80 percent of people in our churches today decided to follow Jesus before age 18; 50 percent of them decided to follow Jesus before age 12.* Not only do most people decide to follow Jesus as children, but statistically it appears that it becomes exponentially more rare and difficult for a person to decide to follow Christ after age 18.[1]

This shouldn't really surprise us. In a statement that Jesus must have known would end up on the wall of virtually every children's ministry in the world, He said, "Let the little children come to me and do not hinder them, for to such belongs the kingdom of heaven" (Matt. 19:14, *ESV*). Jesus wasn't just commenting on what adults need to do to enter the kingdom of heaven, or even giving insight into what the kingdom of heaven is all about; Jesus was telling us something fundamental about childhood.

> Childhood is a season in a person's life when he or she is most open to learning what it means to trust God.

Many people call this spiritual season the 4-14 Window (ages 4 through 14). I don't think this season is by accident. When God said, "For everything there is a season, and a time for every matter under heaven" (Eccles. 3:1, *ESV*), I think He really did mean *everything.* It is during this season of a person's life that we need to focus our efforts on helping that person place his or her trust in Jesus. It's a window of opportunity in the lives of people when they are more moldable than they will ever be in their lifetime. It's when they are forming their understanding of the world, of relationships, of love, of God. It's a season when people are impressionable. We should be intentional about ensuring that each child gets the right impression. What we do during this window may be the most important thing the church does.

While the 4-14 Window represents the reason that children ought to be the number-one priority of your church, it is not the only vital season in a person's life. Much has been done to further the cause of teaching people in age-appropriate ways. In the last 100 years, the church has done a good job of adopting some of the most relevant research on developmental stages and human development. We know this is important because we recognize that if we are to capture the imagination of the child with the timeless message of the gospel, we must communicate in ways a child understands at each age level. We know that each age level has different characteristics that we ignore at our own peril. I believe that there are also vital spiritual seasons connected to each major developmental stage in a person's life that are at least as significant, if not more significant, than the developmental stage itself. This is based upon two key principles of spiritual formation.

Principles of Spiritual Formation

Principle #1: Spiritual Formation Builds upon Itself

In the same way that each developmental stage builds upon itself, spiritual formation builds upon itself. We learn to crawl before we walk; we learn to walk before we run. The same is true when it comes to spiritual matters. There appear to be three major spiritual seasons before a person becomes an adult. Roughly, they are preschool, elementary and youth. The following information was inspired by the ministry and philosophy of Henrietta Mears and is given in more detail in her book *Sunday School Changes Everything*.

Preschool

During this developmental stage, what is learned is largely based upon the impressions received from the world around us. The age characteristic is best represented by the word "absorption." Preschoolers build their conception of the world by absorbing information from the world around them. Spiritually speaking, we learn what love is from those most connected to us (our parents, our teachers, our family) before we learn what God's love is like. Most of this happens before age five. Children absorb their understanding of love from their most significant relationships. This understanding will shape their conception of God's love that they will carry with them through adulthood. This spiritual season is best characterized by the word "impress." Our efforts should focus on giving a first impression of God's character.

Impress: Giving a first impression of God's character

Elementary

There are two major developmental stages happening during the elementary years. They are best represented by the words "activity" (ages 6-8) and "energy" (ages 9-11). This is probably obvious for those of us who work with elementary-age kids. They learn best when moving and actively engaged in the learning process. Because we know this is the time when most people are going to make a decision to follow Jesus, our focus needs to be on the gospel message. This spiritual season is best characterized by the word "trust." Our efforts should focus on helping kids place their trust in Christ and develop a faith in a God bigger than anything they might face.

Trust: Helping kids place their trust in Christ and develop a faith in a God bigger than anything they might face

Youth

There are three major developmental stages taking place during the youth years. They are best represented by the words "adjustment" (middle school), "aspiration" (high school), and "self-confidence" (college). This period spans ages 12–25. It is during this spiritual season that most people will decide how much of their life they will surrender to Jesus. They may have made a decision to follow Jesus as a child, but their experiences during this season will shape the quality of that "followership." Consequently, most people in ministry today trace their calling to something that happened between the ages of 12 and 25, which simply means that most of the future leaders of the church are in our children's and student ministries today. This spiritual season is best characterized by the word "ignite." Our efforts should focus on helping youth discover their role in the kingdom of God and igniting a passion for service.

Ignite: Helping youth discover their role in the kingdom of God and igniting a passion for service

Because preschoolers, elementary-age kids and youth are so dramatically different, it is easy for us to build programs, curriculums, departments and ministries around each age and miss how each of these stages builds upon the previous ones. We must remember that we are not ministering to preschoolers, elementary-age kids and students, but that we are ministering to people who are going to spend a small but pivotal slice of their lives as a preschooler, as an elementary-age kid and as a student. God is going to do something very unique during each season that will be the foundation upon which the next season is built.

> Just because a phase of life is brief and is replaced by another more sophisticated, we should not rush past it; for if we bypass the unique stages of childhood, we strip each succeeding developmental stage of some of its finest ingredients.[2]

This why it is vital for ministry leaders to work across departmental lines to formulate a plan for the spiritual formation of the whole person in light of what God is doing uniquely in each spiritual season. When we recognize that we are dealing with people, lack of cooperation between children's and student ministries becomes inexcusable. We must work together if we are to work with how God has hardwired spiritual formation.

Principle #2: What Is Rooted in the Heart of a Child Is Almost Impossible to Uproot in the Life of an Adult

What happens in childhood can be a force for good or, as we know, it can be a force for bad. Things that are malformed in childhood have repercussions that grow bigger as we grow older. How many adults are wrestling with doubts about God's love for them because of something they experienced in their childhood? The opposite is also true: Foundations that are well laid also have a growing impact for good as a person grows older.

We see this play out most dramatically when we look at the difference between how adults come to know Christ and how most children come to know Christ. Most adults come to know Christ through brokenness. For many adults, it takes a pivotal circumstance (the death of a loved one, a divorce, a bankruptcy, major illness, loss of a job, a prodigal child, marital problems, struggles with addiction, and so on) in order to see their need for God. In fact, it seems that most spiritual growth in adulthood comes through pain. C. S. Lewis once wrote, "Pain is God's megaphone. God whispers in our pleasures, but he shouts in our pain."[3] It's painful to re-form foundations—sometimes you have to tear down walls in order to get to the foundation. In adulthood, that's exactly what we are doing; we are trying to change the foundation after the building is already built.

Children do not usually come to Christ through brokenness. They don't have a significant amount of life experience to be in that position. They come to Christ through relationships with mature Christian adults who are invested in their lives. Henrietta Mears used to say, "First I learned to love my teacher, then I learned to love my teacher's God."[4]

This gives new meaning to what Jesus said at the end of the sermon on the mount: "He who hears these words of mine and does them will be like a wise man who built his house upon the rock" (Matt. 7:24, *ESV*). Adults are in the process of tearing down the house they built upon the sand, in order to rebuild their house upon the rock. With children, we have the opportunity to work with God in laying a foundation upon the rock and help them avoid the pain of rebuilding later on. What if we were intentional about rooting in every person, at an early age, trust in a heavenly Father who loves them no matter what? Children's ministry is setting an anchor in the heart of each child. When they grow up, they will have had such an experience of God's love that it will be difficult to drift from it.

However, in many churches, what is happening in children's and student ministry is woefully undersupported by and invisible to the rest of the church. This is nothing new. Nearly 60 years ago, Henrietta Mears said:

> When you look at most churches—their programming, their staff, and their budgets—it appears that children must first become prodigals, then we will go about putting together elaborate programs and events to save them.[5]

Let's face it, many of us who have been in children's ministry for a while recognize that most church leaders view children's ministry as the opportunity cost of ministering to adults. How many times have we heard church leaders reassuring us that children's ministry is important: "You know, if we don't have a great children's ministry we won't reach their parents"? At what point is someone going to stand up and say what Jesus said: "Stop turning the children away; they're people too! In fact, they are better at making the decision to follow Me than the rest of you" (see Matt. 19:14)?

One of the biggest dangers we are facing in the church right now is that we might be responsible for passing down to the next generation a false model. We have trained the next generation to believe that real ministry is with adults, and just about anything for children will do. As a result, we pretty much ensure that our recovery ministries will be full of people who are the product of failed children's ministries of the previous generation. I know this is a harsh perspective, but I think it is corroborated by the fact that somewhere between 60 percent and 80 percent of children who grow up in our churches walk away from their faith and a vital connection to the church within two years of graduating from high school.[6] This doesn't account for the many millions of boys and girls who never cross the threshold of a church at all. If a pool had those statistics, we would shut it down!

Many of these students are walking away from the church during the very season God has designed to capture their hearts for His kingdom. A recent *Wall Street Journal* article gave us this alarming view:

> Surveys always find that younger people are less likely to attend church, yet this has never resulted in the decline of the churches. It merely reflects the fact that, having left home, many single young

adults choose to sleep in on Sunday mornings. . . . Once they marry, though, and especially once they have children, their attendance rates recover. Unfortunately, because the press tends not to publicize this correction, many church leaders continue unnecessarily fretting about regaining the lost young people.[7]

It is this sort of thinking that is exactly what is fundamentally wrong with how we view the spiritual potential of the student ministry season. Students who left church do seem to come back after marriage and kids. However, they largely come back having lost their first love and lacking the revolutionary spirit they had in their youth. They come back as church attenders, not as leaders or Kingdom pioneers. This sort of mentality robs the church of future leaders. Here is a perceptive warning from Christian educator Henrietta Mears:

> The church cannot live for conversion of adult sinners. If it is not to die, it must live for the saving and development of children and young people. The winning of a child to Christ is our most important task today. When we save a child, we not only save a soul, but we gain a life. Children have the right to demand your best leaders, your best materials, your best facilities. Our churches have spent millions in erecting large sanctuaries, in putting in pipe organs and stained-glass windows which are to be enjoyed once a week, but how much has the average church invested in its children, its little children?[8]

Being in ministry, we know that this is not an either/or proposition. But think about this for a moment. Think about all of the money, volunteers and resources we put behind outreach events for adults. What if we reversed that? What could you do in your community if the worship department gave you the Christmas pageant budget? What if all of those countless volunteer hours spent in rehearsals beginning in July (Christmas in July?) were spent praying for children and families, calling and visiting families and their children, and equipping people to become better small-group leaders and Sunday School teachers for all of the families that will show up in the fall? What if the adult Sunday School class that has been meeting for the last 10 years disbanded and took all of that knowledge and wisdom they have acquired and committed to investing in a small group of kids every week for an entire year? Isn't that the kind of small-group leader or Sunday School teacher we all want for our kids?

Unsaved adults will always be among us, and they will need environments designed to reach them; but a person is a child only for a short time. And in that short time, the entire course of a life can be altered.

How many adult problems would be solved if every preschooler who entered our churches left knowing they have a heavenly Father who loves them? Or what if every elementary-age child left knowing that he or she can place his or her trust in Jesus for every area of life? Or what if every high school student left knowing his or her place in God's story and making a lifetime commitment to serve Christ? What if every college ministry developed that calling to life service? What if everything we did for children focused on winning them to Christ?

> God intends that we should win people in the days of their youth while their hearts are young and sensitive. But we are apt to let the springtime pass and then with great effort create a religious fervor by our own efforts and win men to Christ. We work hard, spend thousands of dollars and at the best get disappointingly small returns. We have waited too long. That which we should do is to work with God in His seasons.[9]

Jesus put the child in the midst of His ministry; therefore, we should put the child in the midst of the church. Not only do I believe that God blesses this, but if we were really honest, this would be the most strategic use of our resources and bear the most fruit for the kingdom of God in the future.

We are shaping the future of the church in the children's ministries of today.

What would the next generation look like if a church invested in its youngest members? Would we need as many Christmas pageants and Easter events? Maybe with enough resources we could do VBS every Sunday!

DISCUSSION QUESTONS

1. In your own words, describe the 4-14 Window and its importance for your ministry to children.
2. How do you give your 4-14 Window kids opportunities to place their trust in Jesus? How can you be more intentional in planning these opportunities?
3. Are these opportunities age appropriate? What do you need to change?
4. How can your ministry have an overarching plan that builds a readiness to accept the gospel? List ways you can plan for the following stages: preschool, elementary and youth.
5. How can you improve communication between leaders of the different age levels in your ministry in order to be intentional about cultivating spiritual growth? What training would be helpful?
6. What are the consequences of neglecting to provide children with opportunities to cultivate a personal trust in Jesus and their Lord and Savior? What are the long-term benefits of reaching kids during the 4/14 Window?

Notes
1. The Barna Group, "Evangelism Is Most Effective Among Kids," October 11, 2004. https://www.barna.org/barna-update/article/5-barna-update/196-evangelism-is-most-effective-among-kids#.UjiyRLxMarU.
2. Henrietta C. Mears, *Sunday School Changes Everything* (Ventura, CA: Regal Books, 2012), p. 65.
3. C. S. Lewis, *The Problem of Pain* (New York: HarperOne, 2009), p. 83.
4. Henrietta C. Mears, unpublished archive source.
5. Ibid.
6. Scott McConnell, "LifeWay Research Finds Reasons 18- to 22-Year-Olds Drop Out of Church," *LifeWay*, August 7, 2007. http://www.lifeway.com/Article/LifeWay-Research-finds-reasons-18-to-22-year-olds-drop-out-of-church (accessed October 2013). The Barna Group, "You Lost Me: Why Young Christians Are Leaving Church . . . and Rethinking Faith," November 16, 2011. https://www.barna.org/teens-next-gen-articles/534-five-myths-about-young-adult-church-dropouts (accessed October 2013).
7. Rodney Stark and Byron Johnson, "Religion and the Bad News Bearers," *Wall Street Journal* (August 26, 2011).
8. Henrietta Mears, unpublished archive source.
9. Arthur Gage, *Evangelism of Youth* (Philadelphia: Judson Press, 1922), p. 10.

3

Threads: Weaving Jesus into the Lives of the Next Generation

DONNA LUCAS

Donna Lucas is a pastor's daughter at heart. She left a life of big-budget fashion and world travel to serve children's ministry leaders through her work as Gospel Light's publishing director. Her passion for Jesus and the next generation fire her efforts, while her perspectives flow from a unique mix of business knowledge and serious study of Jesus' leadership principles. She speaks to children's ministry leaders each week, learning from them and advising them. She's a wife, a sports mom and the volunteer children's ministry coordinator at her church in Newbury Park, California. She loves kids and delights in helping leaders successfully draw kids to Jesus and help them grow in lifelong relationship with Him.

God Can Use Anyone!

If anyone had told me eight years ago that I might write a chapter for a book on children's ministry, I would have choked with laughter. You see, I'm a veteran of the fashion industry—second only to entertainment in its reputation for being viciously cutthroat. But amazingly, God used it to train me for children's ministry! Each day I see more clearly how He used my experiences in the fashion world to prepare me in ways I never could have imagined if I hadn't experienced it firsthand.

Leaving the fashion industry was a leap of faith into the unknown for me. But God used my "unknowing" to help me learn to rely on Him more deeply than ever. We've all had those moments when we realize that God is calling us to something huge—and suddenly we see how it is *all* about relying on Him to make us effective, creative and strong. In fact, I sometimes wonder, *Did God place me here to lead kids to Jesus—or to learn to seek Him more deeply?* Perhaps it is both! Certainly, while writing this chapter, I've remembered God's faithfulness in my own story and been drawn to seek Him more.

A Pivotal Point

So why, you may ask, is a former fashion executive so fired up about children's ministry? Let me tell you. I have three beautiful daughters. When the youngest was entering middle school, and the eldest her sophomore year in college, I thought I could kick back a little—after all, this was my third time through sixth grade! But I also knew I had just a year or two in which to help solidify my youngest daughter's faith before she entered high school. She had accepted Jesus; I expected that now we just had to work on strengthening her relationship with Him. But what I didn't expect was how much sixth grade had changed!

As I watched my youngest study Early Civilizations, I realized that her understanding about the Bible and Jesus' place in it was more important than ever. The textbooks were just plain wrong about Jewish history. I often pulled out my Bible so that we could compare it with her textbook. But her eyes told me that she was wondering, *Who is telling me the truth—teacher or Mom? Textbook or Bible? Is there really only one truth?*

I was shocked that my daughter had to wrestle so hard at such a young age; I thought school should still be pretty carefree! But Early Civilizations showed me two things: first, the importance of her developing a strong relationship with Jesus; and second, the limited window for developing that relationship. (I know, I should have started sooner!)

When my eldest entered sixth grade, public schools were fairly subtle in their agenda. Ten years and two daughters later, nothing is subtle about it. Much of what we adults know as history is not only politically incorrect—it isn't even mentioned! As early as sixth grade, kids in our public schools have teachers who challenge any Christian belief as intolerant, uneducated or just "not smart."

So all of this has made me ask myself, *What can we do to help our kids understand truth? What will make the difference for the next generation?* And as much as kids need to understand what truth is, they need even more to have more than *knowledge about* Jesus. *Do the kids in our churches know Jesus—the Way, the Truth and the Life?* They need a *personal relationship with* Him.

Truth, Spirit and Teacher

In public speaking, I learned to slow down and look to gauge the reaction of my crowd. Yet, when I teach kids, I can forget to do just that. I can be so wrapped up in the schedule that I forget to see if the kids are engaged—and what's more, it's easy to become so focused on games and activities that I don't slow down and wait for the Lord! You see, when He takes over the classroom, things may get messy, off schedule and almost always bring a hard question or two. Yet, on the Sundays when I give the classroom to His Spirit and allow Him to lead me to speak to those children, I see that more was accomplished than Bible learning alone; the kids also gained a stronger relationship with Jesus.

In fact, it's largely through my relationship with Jesus that these kids will learn to love Him. While this may sound arrogant, hear me out. First of all, "more is caught than is taught." It's not that I am more important to God than those 11 little kids or that I am some kind of master teacher. But I do believe that my passion for Jesus, for them and for inviting God into their class time means that I can trust God to use me to speak His truth into their lives. And that does make me important. Henrietta Mears said that if we were professors at Harvard, we'd probably be glad to let everyone know what an important job we were doing. But this? This is the most important teaching job on planet Earth! God values what He does through us—and so should we.

Key Components to a Jesus-Centered Ministry

In ministry today, many of us feel like we're just getting by—we manage to get the basics done. But we can do the same old same old, week after week without knowing where we are going. A clear vision is necessary for good leadership; but often, we don't know where to start the process. All leadership starts with vision. In the rest of this chapter, we will look at six key components that will help you gain clear vision for creating a unique, Jesus-centered ministry that will weave Jesus' words, life and power into the fabric of your kids' lives.

1. Understand Relevance

"Relevant" is a word that gets thrown around a lot—it's often used to make us feel out of touch or inferior! (When I looked up the word on Merriam Webster, I found that it is in the top 1 percent of all the words searched—maybe because it is so . . . relevant?) Being relevant in ministry doesn't mean buying a smart phone and a tablet, or new apps. Relevance is a way of interacting. It arises from an understanding of current culture; however, it doesn't mean falling into every trend. Instead, being relevant means that we keep a steady eye on what matters and then use current culture to engage people and guide them to Jesus.

2. Recognize Defining Moments

Every generation is defined by significant moments—whether inspiring or scary. These moments change the way we see our lives. Consider a defining moment from your own life; it's likely an event that moved you and changed your worldview.

Mine came in five words that still chill me: "Challenger, go at throttle up." It was a major world event that left me thinking, *I must be an adult now.* MTV also defined my generation; I remember hearing how we were going to be destroyed, and MTV would be the culprit. But for those of us with a healthy relationship with Jesus, MTV was merely entertainment, because we'd already had our most defining moment—meeting Jesus!

This current generation (like every other) will be defined by their own unique events; but it's good for us to remember that, for them, 9/11 won't have much meaning—it's history, not experience, for them! Whether it is a political moment like the election of the first African American president, a cause like ending slavery, or the fear that rises from shootings in schools and movie theaters, knowing what defines these kids will help us relate and communicate with them. (And of course, that means we must click, scroll and slide it, as well as know the technology heroes like Steve Jobs and Mark Zuckerberg.)

But even for the most technologically challenged of us, it's good to know that some things don't change: The best way to get to know this generation is still to hang out with them—and the bonus is that they can often solve our tech issues (and we learn the lingo and the shortcuts). This became really clear to me when I was trying to explain to my husband that it's no longer a pound sign (#); it's a hashtag. (When I listen to preteens, they move so fast that I have learned to wait until the end of the thought when they add the hashtag, which usually sums it all up!)

3. Develop Your Volunteers

One of the most important parts of our ministry is our volunteers—people who understand the value of what they do, who know God has called them to this work, and who are passionate about helping kids know Jesus. That's our dream description. But as more people work full time, and as their lives become busier, we find people looking to Sunday as a day to attend church, drink in whatever encouragement they can, and spend the rest of the day for their families and themselves, whether that means sports, running errands or a holy nap! Many don't see themselves as having time for volunteering or teaching in children's ministry.

A Barna survey of senior pastors indicated that this attitude is basically a vision problem. This attitude (based on a thousand different factors) creates a huge challenge for everyone in the church, from senior pastor to teen volunteer! It affects the quality of what our kids learn, how they grow spiritually and what kind of spiritual leader they become. Basically, it boils down to this: If our generation doesn't value kids and kids' ministry *now*, we're telling the kids they don't matter. Then, they will grow up not only with less understanding, but also with an attitude that kids aren't important, and teaching them doesn't matter. The ripple effect can destroy succeeding generations as well!

We all know that's the problem, but what's the solution? We have to *evangelize*! But, important as that is, I'm not talking about outsiders. We need to evangelize our own people! When you have effectively shared your vision, people will get excited. They will commit to work when they are committed to the vision. More than that, when their minds and hearts are engaged in your vision, their ears are open to God's call to them! If you do not establish vision and calling, volunteering then tends to come out of a sense of duty or guilt. Those volunteers fall away, burn out and give up. They won't be as committed as you are—because commitment will make all the difference.

Once we have volunteers who are committed and know God's call, we have to *establish* them. The word "establish" means to bring about permanent change. Think about this in terms of your own salvation. You were first evangelized. You received God's message of salvation through Jesus and you decided to accept it; yet, without the establishing of your faith into permanent life change, you were still prey to Satan, as Paul tells us in Colossians:

> But now he has reconciled you by Christ's physical body through death to present you holy in his sight, without blemish and free from accusation—if you continue in your faith, established and firm, and do not move from the hope held out in the gospel. This is the gospel that you heard and that has been proclaimed to every creature under heaven, and of which I, Paul, have become a servant (Col. 1:22-23).

This Scripture tells us how important it is for us to be not just saved, but also firm and unmoving from our faith. This is also the way you want your volunteers to believe in your vision for ministry and to be fully committed to the calling that God has given them.

Next you must *equip* your leaders—train them because you value them, you value kids and, most of all, you value God's glory in the whole ministry. You may have outstanding ideas to take these committed volunteers and make great teachers, but first, you have to get them to attend training sessions! That becomes the hardest part.

We must be very creative to get the attention of our teams. It is important to train them about the curriculum you are using (that might come together in a pizza party or a Saturday morning coffee party). Part of having a Jesus-centered ministry means we mentor and act as spiritual leaders to our volunteers. We do our best to help our volunteers experience their own encounters with Jesus; we work to help them find God's purpose for them. A true spiritual leader will influence more than direct, and inspire more than instruct. Be that kind of leader.

But I believe the most effective equipping is done one on one. In the same way that Jesus mentored the disciples, we need to be in mentorship with our volunteers. When in tune to their needs and weaknesses, we can then offer resources, Scripture and encouragement that are right for them. I like to think of it as training snacks—not the food kind; but little portions of training will help your volunteers stay engaged from week to week, month to month and throughout the year!

For effective equipping, we need to know our volunteers. Even when it's easier to run off to the next thing, letting people know that you will be around for debriefing after a Sunday School or kids' event means that you can engage in frequent conversations that happen when the need or idea is freshest in the mind of that volunteer! Here are some of the practical questions I use with my team:

- What was the best thing that happened in your class? What part was hardest—activity? storytelling?
- In what ways did you see God's fingerprints on the class this week? Tell me about it.
- What was your biggest challenge today? Biggest challenge this past week?
- Know their family situation: How is your husband? Wife? Kids? How did Jacob do in his baseball game this week?
- What can I do to serve you this week? What do you need from me?

Just as in our questions to kids, we need to focus on open-ended conversation starters here so that we get not only an answer but also hear the hearts of these marvelous people! As I read blogs, magazines, books and resources, I gather training snacks that I can use whenever one of my volunteers needs a quick idea, a spiritual lift or advice on a problem. When I know my volunteers, it's easy to be personal in my training efforts and really hit the mark with my team.

Most of us know that we have to train our teams to be the best teachers possible, but if you hear nothing else I say, please hear this: Do *not* forget the most important part of training: how to lead kids to the salvation decision! Let me tell you why.

Last summer at our VBS, our worship leader asked if anyone was interested in accepting Jesus as their Savior. To my surprise, children began coming to the front. As I made my way to the front to talk to them, I watched my volunteers back up and move away. I was shocked—but then I realized that *none* of them felt comfortable talking to the kids about joining God's family and following Jesus Christ. At this crucial time, when God had moved in kids' hearts, I had left the workers in the field unprepared. (Yes, that was a defining moment for me!)

Do you train your leaders to talk to your children about what it means to follow Jesus? How they can join God's family forever? Do they know how to identify a child who is truly ready and understands the decision he or she is making? Or when the time comes, do they seek you out so that *you* can have a conversation with that child? The most important training session you can have is the one that will make your team most uncomfortable—and it is the one that may well have the most eternal impact. This is another aspect of training that might best be reinforced one on one. When you and a volunteer or two are at coffee, pull out some kids' evangelism booklets. Ask them what they would say. Do a little role-play, with you as the child. Give them confidence that God is the one who saves people and they need only to present Jesus and let the Spirit of God do the rest.

We can learn a lot from the way Jesus developed His disciples. Throughout the Gospels, Jesus invited people to come with Him and see for themselves the power of God. When the disciples spent time with Jesus, they observed how He handled Himself and the words He spoke, and they learned every step of the way. Jesus wove His life into theirs. Let your volunteers observe you and your best leaders.

Always keep an eye out for developing the next leader. Jesus chose Peter, James and John to come on special tasks with Him. They were His helpers, the ones He looked to for support in time of need. As you observe leaders who are growing, take them with you, give them opportunities to pray or speak or counsel alongside you and to you. As they experience the power of God, their level of joy and commitment will increase their desire to step up to a leadership role. Let your leaders experience the power of God in your ministry.

When your leaders are ready, give them assignments—Jesus did. We read in the Gospels that when confronted with more than 5,000 hungry followers, the disciples wanted to send the crowd away. Jesus turned the problem over to them and gave them the opportunity to get creative by telling them to give the crowd something to eat!

"We have here only five loaves of bread and two fish," they answered (Matt. 14:17).

And when they had no ideas (which means it was a teachable moment!), Jesus took what they had, gave thanks and gave directions as to how to distribute the coming miracle. Looking up to heaven, He gave thanks and broke the loaves. Then He gave them to the disciples, and the disciples gave them to the people (see Matt. 14:16-19).

Jesus empowered them to come up with an idea. Jesus used their little amount of food, supplied the miracle and allowed the disciples to be part of it. Face to face with the crowd, the disciples experienced the miracle and then had the opportunity to point these people to the fact that Jesus was the Son of God. Jesus put His disciples in the situation to interact with the people. He was interested in seeing who His followers were becoming.

We all need to see God at work in the hearts of the children we serve. Put your leaders face to face with the children—it's what makes you come back when you're having a tough time, so let it motivate them! The sweet little comments, the aha moments, center us and remind us why we do what we do.

Let me tell you just one more story. Along with the others, Hannah had been memorizing the books of the Bible, part of a program to help us monitor our children's progress in learning. One Sunday, five-year-old Hannah went to one of our volunteers and said she had memorized the names of all 66 books of the Bible. Her teacher was so excited that she brought Hannah to me. We both listened to her recite the names of the books with her precious little lisp: "Genesis, Esodis, Viticus, Numbuz, Deutomonomy . . ." Tears welled up in our eyes as she flawlessly went through the Old Testament, then the New Testament, then repeated them a second time. My teacher was so excited! She said, "Do you trust me? I want to do something radical here." I said, "Yes."

She looked at Hannah and said, "Come on, Hannah, let's go to Big Church." She marched Hannah right to the front of the service and interrupted the pastor, whispering in his ear. To my surprise he gave her the stage. She turned to Hannah and said, "Hannah, can you tell them what you just told me and Miss Donna?"

Hannah began, "Genesis, Esodis, Viticus, Numbuz, Deutomonomy . . ." There was not a dry eye in the place! She hugged Hannah and told the audience, "I get to see how God moves in the hearts of these kids each week. If you think what we do is just childcare, you are wrong. Can *you* say all 66 books of the Bible?"

Talk about a great recruiting day! But more than that, it was the turning point for that teacher. It was a moment that God used to give her a rock-solid commitment to the ministry. I gave her an assignment; she experienced the power of God in this little girl and gained confidence in her ability to lead little ones to Jesus.

4. Build Relationship

Relationship is what God's kingdom is all about. We were created to crave relationship. We were created to have a relationship with God. Human beings must be in relationship to exist. It is how God programmed us. Christ died for relationship. He died and rose again so that we might live through Him, in relationship to His heavenly Father, and then also have relationship here on earth, through the power of the Holy Spirit, with other Christians. It is the essence of His kingdom. It is through relationship that God transforms lives.

If we are looking at the culture around our kids each day, we cannot help but notice that we are raising a culture of loners. All technology has its pros and cons, but if you ask a preteen what his or her most valuable possession is, it would most likely be his or her phone. Our kids are experiencing a new form of relationship—virtual relationship. Face-to-face conversations are secondary to Snapchat and Instagram. Their style of communication is different, and kids are learning it at ever-younger ages. We may be creating a culture of kids that do not have social skills, and I fear that this will backfire in serious relationship issues as they become adults. But look at the opportunity we have as the church in this!

Building relationship is one of the most crucial steps in creating a Jesus-centered ministry. With children, relationships are driven through consistency. Consistency builds trust. Now, I know that your biggest challenge may be getting consistent volunteers; it's certainly my biggest task in ministry. However, that does not change the fact that children need to see the same person week after week in their classroom. That is a crucial first step!

The second step is ensuring that our classes and small-group time with the children focuses more on relationship building than merely on activities. In a Jesus-centered ministry, we are to be models for the child to imitate. Paul wrote in his letter to the Corinthian church, "Follow my example, as I follow the example of Christ" (see 1 Cor. 11:1).

It is our job to show children what it means to be a follower of Christ. We do that through consistency and transparency. When we are consistent, children get to know us. They appreciate our smiles, hugs, laughter; and they learn the way we will react to difficult or surprising situations. These things speak volumes about what it means to be a Christian. Dr. Henrietta Mears said, "First I learned to love my teacher, then I learned to love my teacher's God."[1] That is how God works. He works through our relationships to change lives.

5. Start with a Plan

What would happen if we all had to take a test on the Bible? Do you think you would pass? As I talk to secondary educators at some of our best Christian colleges, I hear the same story over and over. Those freshmen don't even have an elementary understanding of the Bible. Many believe it is a lack of time in the Word alone with God. Others believe it is society's fault. (Isn't that just like us? It's always someone else's fault. After all, we coined the term "no-fault"—so it can't be our own fault! It must be the media's fault, the corporate marketer's fault, evil youth sports programs' fault.)

But we have come to this low level of learning mainly because we stopped teaching the Bible to our kids. It's that simple. For some time, it's been popular to present the Bible as if it's cotton candy (tastes great and melts away fast). Some programs jump from one Bible story to another, teaching topically rather than teaching the Bible as one story.

But the Bible *is* one story, not a random 66 books of moral tales! Jumping from Genesis to Jeremiah to Romans to Ruth doesn't help kids to see the big picture and gain knowledge of the complete story: God's story of His plan to send Jesus to redeem sinful mankind.

When a program jumps around, it's mainly because of our "What can I do next?" way of planning (or not planning!). When we plan, we need consistent goals for what to teach kids at each stage and through each season of their souls; in other words, what we teach needs to help kids understand the Bible both intellectually and in ways that are appropriate to their spiritual understanding.

When you look for a plan, make sure that it is developed for the age of the children—according to their ability to understand—and works with the next level of development. If you know what you want your preteens to know and understand, and you have a picture in your mind of how deep that faith must go, then you know you have to start at nursery and preschool to lay that foundation.

I believe that a complete plan to cover the Bible thoroughly and systematically will eliminate the hopeless confusion and unending repetition of the same stories that breed boredom. The church is giving up its role as educator for fun, baby-sitting, events, field trips and to mentor parents. Nothing is wrong with any of these things, except when they become the complete focus. We can all agree that there is nothing wrong with the Textbook! So if that's true, then it must be in the way we have presented the great facts and teaching of the Book that has become the problem.

It hurts to hear children say things like, "When I don't have to, I'll never go back to Sunday School. There's nothing there for me." But listen to what this child is actually saying! We interpret this to mean that it wasn't fun, or it was boring. But that is not what I hear: I hear the heart of a child who never grew a love for the Bible, who never learned how profoundly it gives us the answer to our problems, and who doesn't have relationship with Jesus or with others that has given value to being at Sunday School.

We all want to blame the evil marketing executives at large entertainment companies or the professors in colleges for dragging our kids away; but as one who was a marketing executive dragging kids into the culture, I can tell you, it's not their fault! It means that we're failing to give our kids love for God's Word, delight in a relationship with Jesus, or the ability to give an answer for their faith.

6. Develop Urgency in Your Ministry

Shortly after I joined Gospel Light, I was in St. Louis at a roundtable of children's ministry leaders. During a conversation with the children's director from a large church in St. Louis, I realized what it meant to have an urgent ministry. As my friend told me all about the issues of his inner city church (broken homes, dads in prison, drug- and gang-infested neighborhoods, shootings, stabbings and violence at every turn), I realized these were things that my suburban church did not experience. Yet, I heard in his voice an excitement for ministry that I didn't have. Through an after-school program at the schools, he spent seven days a week engaging with kids. He told me that no one volunteers unless he or she is trained and willing to personally lead a child to Christ. He said that no child left his presence without hearing the good news about Jesus and being asked if he or she wanted to become a member of God's family. Every child, every service, every event, every chance encounter in his community could be that child's last opportunity. He was intentional because he never knew if he would see that child again.

Most of us feel a little more secure about our environment than that—thus, we do not live in a world with that kind of urgency. But I believe we need that kind of urgency in our desire to lead kids to Jesus, because the world certainly has that kind of urgency in keeping our kids from the saving grace of Jesus. It is a battle, and the question remains: Who is going to win the battle for our kids?

In his book *Transforming Children into Spiritual Champions*, George Barna presents research that shows us that we have about a 34 percent chance of a child between the ages of 5 and 12 becoming a Christian. If that seems like we are fighting a losing battle, consider this: between 13 and 18, there is a 4 percent chance that a person will accept Christ.[2] That makes children's ministry feel like I have the most opportunity for success! That reality changes things. Let's add to that reality; in looking at our family I estimate that:

- Between birth and 13 years of age there are 113,880 hours in a child's life; 38,000 hours are reserved for sleeping.
- At 6 hours a day for about 100 days a year, kids aged 5 to 13 spend 9,720 hours in school.
- The average kid consumes a minimum of 25 hours of media a week. That's 16,900 hours of time to influence that child's heart through media.
- If we can get the kids to church for 2 hours a week, and they come every week (highly unlikely, I know, but let's be optimistic), the church gets 1,352 hours.

Mom and Dad get the rest. That is 47,908 hours.

Of course, parents have more time, but the question is, "What are we, the church, going to do with those 1,300 hours?" It had better be meaningful and intentional, and it had better be *serious* business.

In the newly released book *Sunday School Changes Everything*, Henrietta Mears says that Sunday School is big business because it is God's business. She goes on to say, "Those who run big businesses may be dealing with millions or billions of dollars, but time will bring that all to an end. What we are doing is of eternal significance. We are preparing lives not only for this world but for the world that is to come. We must be impressed with the magnitude of our task."[3] She knew the importance of the work that we all still do. There is a reason that recent research shows that 92 percent of churches in America still run a Sunday School program for their children.[4] It is a meaningful, intentional ministry that bears fruit.

When we build a Jesus-centered ministry, we are creating a ministry that is built upon a desire to be relevant to kids and their families. It is a ministry that evangelizes, establishes and equips volunteers according to their skills and calling—just as Jesus developed His disciples. It is a ministry that creates relationship with the children and teaches by example, as Jesus taught. A Jesus-centered ministry starts with a plan that points kids to the whole of Scripture as pointing to Jesus, the Way, the Truth and the Life. Finally a Jesus-centered ministry is urgent. In the 1940s, Henrietta Mears said, "Our children are on the auction block being sold to the highest bidder."[5] That is even more likely today than in any previous generation.

But to me, this is the most compelling reason to create a Jesus-centered ministry: Our kids need a strong relationship with Jesus Christ to carry them through the challenges of the teen years, young adulthood and the rest of their lives.

If my daughter Kelly had not been questioning as she did in sixth grade, I might not have become so passionate about developing not just the knowledge of Bible stories but also helping kids develop a stronger relationship with Jesus. It's not such a long way from fashion—now it's my passion to weave the words, the power and the love of Jesus into kids' lives and see those amazing tapestries of grace fly in the breeze!

DISCUSSION QUESTIONS

1. Picture your fifth- to sixth-graders. List 10 things you want them to know/ believe/embrace before you turn them over to the youth leaders.

   1.
   2.
   3.
   4.
   5.
   6.
   7.
   8.
   9.
   10.

2. Take some time to gather your church mission or vision statement. Compare it to your ministry vision. Do the two visions support each other? ___ YES ___ NO
3. Describe the similarities:
4. Note any points that differ between your vision and your church's vision:
5. If you do not have a ministry vision, try to create one sentence that defines what you will accomplish. (Example: Our children's ministry team is dedicated to drawing kids to Jesus and leading them in a life-long relationship with Him.)
6. Spend some time with your older elementary-age kids. Ask them to tell you who their favorite celebrities are. Make a list and write the names here:
7. Are you familiar with all of them? If so, put a check mark; if not, Google them and find out who they are.
8. Now Google them and see how many search results you get for each one. It will tell you how popular and culturally significant they are.
9. Find the scope and sequence (teaching plan) for all of the curriculum you use, from preschool to preteen. Compare the plans and be sure they make sense in leading children to your ultimate goal. Will they accomplish the 10 qualities you want your preteens to have? Yes or No. List here what is missing:
10. How many children in your ministry accepted Jesus last year?

11. How many teachers do you believe are comfortable leading a child to Christ?
12. Brainstorm with yourself or with your team three ways you can create more urgency within your team.

Notes
1. Henrietta Mears, unpublished archive source.
2. George Barna, *Transforming Children into Spiritual Champions* (Ventura, CA: Gospel Light, 2003), p. 39.
3. Henrietta C. Mears, *Sunday School Changes Everything* (Ventura, CA: Regal Books, 2010), p. 31.
4. Barna Group, "State of Sunday School," *2010 Pastor's Poll.*
5. Henrietta Mears, unpublished archive source.

PART 2:

How to Build Your Ministry on the Gospel

4

The Seven Factors in a Gospel-Centered Ministry

STEVE ADAMS

Steve Adams has been the children's pastor at Saddleback Church in Southern California since 2007. He has served as a children's pastor for over 20 years and is a leader and mentor to many children's ministry leaders around the country and into the world. God has blessed him with a creative mind, a true pastor's heart and a passion for serving God and others through children's ministry! Steve and his wife, Stephanie, have two sons: Tyler and Matthew.

When I was a child, my mom always told me that it is not nice to point. As a kid, it is hard to understand why. If you see something that you want someone else to see, you point it out. Well, this is fine as long as it is an inanimate object like a building, place of interest or scenery. But it is not nice to point at people.

Now, as a mature adult (my wife would argue that claim), I can clearly see how pointing at a person can be misinterpreted. Most people do not like to be singled out, and pointing at them does just that. But the reality is, Scripture does that too. It points at someone. The totality of Scripture points to Jesus—the Author and Finisher of our faith, the Prince of Peace, the Redeemer of mankind, the Great Shepherd, and the Savior of the world. From the sacrificial system of the Old Testament to the prophecies of Revelation, it all points to Jesus.

Jesus said, "You search the Scriptures because you believe they give you eternal life. But the Scriptures point to me!" (John 5:39, *NLT*). No matter what your starting point is in the Scriptures, it will point you to Jesus the Savior. Why? Because Jesus, the "good news," is the center. "Then Jesus quoted passages from the writings of Moses and all the prophets, explaining what all the Scriptures said about himself" (Luke 24:27, *NLT*).

He came as the Word of God in the flesh. He *is* the gospel. He literally is "the good news." The good news is the central force that drove everything: the healings, the teachings and the miracles. At the center of all of this, we find the gospel of Jesus Christ.

Jesus' objective was to seek and save those who were lost: "For the Son of Man came to seek and save those who are lost" (Luke 19:10, *NLT*).

Jesus *is* the good news. He *is* redemption. He *is* forgiveness. He *is* our salvation. God had no intention of waving a wand or snapping His fingers and having the world fall into forced submission.

What practical steps did Jesus take to share the good news? Maybe Jesus could have done really cool magic tricks and performed supernatural miracles upon request to show the people that He was God's own Son. Several times throughout Scripture, Jesus said the words "be healed." Why couldn't He simply say the words "be saved" as He waved His hand over the crowds? Well, He could have, but that was not the plan. God did not send Jesus to build a robot army, mechanically following every command because the freedom of choice had been eradicated and replaced with mindless reflexes.

In God's plan, He would present Himself to the world through Jesus and offer them a choice. He chose this path because He wanted us to truly love Him.

Jesus' objective as the gospel—the good news—was and is to seek and save those who are lost. Those words may have been concise, but it was not simple. There were many components to sharing the good news. Jesus not only had to teach effectively, but He also had to establish relationships, build teams and mentor leaders. Sounds a lot like children's ministry, doesn't it?

In this book, we are exploring the idea of having a gospel-centered children's ministry. Throughout Scripture, everywhere you look, you see the writer pointing directly to Jesus. He is the Messiah and the fulfillment of prophecy. Every story and every event points to the gospel of Jesus, the center of Scripture.

So how does all of this connect to us as a children's ministry leader? Think about this: If you have ever been in a canoe, you understand the importance of the "center." As long as you are in the center of the boat, you are fine. But the moment you lean to one side or the other, you can feel the boat leaning in that direction. If you lean too far to one side, you will tip the boat over. If you want to stay in the canoe and out of the water, you must stay in the center of the boat.

With that in mind, let me ask you this question: Since Jesus, as the good news, is the center of Scripture, how is Jesus also the center of our ministry to children?

Our ministries are gospel-centered when our methodology, approach and structure point back to the central theme or objective of Scripture—of sharing the good news, Jesus. And just like Jesus' ministry while here on earth, this may be a concise objective, but it is far from simple.

As you are well aware, children's ministry is quite complicated. There are many facets and components that must all work together in harmony for a children's ministry to be successful. Since the gospel of Jesus is the center of Scripture, it would stand to reason that the gospel would be at the center of our children's ministries. But what does that look like?

Jesus' life and ministry give us a blueprint that will help us keep Jesus and the gospel at the center of every component of our ministry to children. There are several factors that were central to Jesus' ministry that if implemented in our own leadership and ministries will be greatly beneficial as well. These seven factors include (1) the Calling Factor, (2) the Compass Factor, (3) the

Connection Factor, (4) the Choice Factor, (5) the Courage Factor, (6) the Creativity Factor, and (7) the Commitment Factor.

1. The Calling Factor

Jesus knew *why* He was coming to earth, and it was that acute understanding of why He was here that kept Him on track when it would have been much easier to quit. In the deepest part of His anguish, He could have called it quits. He could have, with a single command, unleashed the fury and wrath of God on those who were tormenting Him. But He did not.

Why? Because He knew why He was here. Jesus knew that coming to earth for the specific purpose of saving humanity was His calling.

How about you? Why are you doing what you do? Wait, let me guess: The pay is outstanding, the benefits are out of this world, the accolades are invigorating, the constant stream of encouragement is too empowering to walk away from, you get your own parking space and, oh, let's not forget all of the Nilla wafers you can eat. Not even close? (Well, except for the Nilla wafer part.)

If you have been in children's ministry for more than five years, you have probably already settled this question for yourself. If you are new to children's ministry, you must settle this issue of calling or you will be out of children's ministry by the time this writing celebrates one year in print. How can I make such a strong assumption? It is because the Calling Factor is the anchor of your ministry.

If you are called to do what you are doing, you will outlast the storms. If you are not called, you will jump ship as soon as the second and third big wave rocks the boat. I am not trying to be sarcastic here; I am speaking from many years of experience. I have watched this drama play out over and over and over again.

I have known people who went into children's ministry because it was the only position available. How long do you think they lasted? Not long. In fact, here is a quick story of just such an example. I was taking an additional Greek class at a seminary near the college I was attending. One afternoon, I stepped into the elevator and headed up to the class. Now, I was only on this campus for the one Greek class. This was not the university I attended, so I did not know anyone on this campus. Okay, back to the elevator. I stepped into the elevator and turned to face the door as is our custom in North America. I could hear the two guys talking behind me even though I tried my best to ignore them. This is exactly the conversation I heard: "So what are you going to do, man?" "Well,

I didn't get the position I wanted at this church, but they are pretty desperate for a children's pastor, so I'll take that job until I graduate, and then I can find a real job [laughter]." "I didn't know you like working with kids." "[laughter] I don't. I just need something to pay the bills while I finish these last two semesters."

As I listened to this conversation, I felt the pressure building like a volcano. Wisdom says it is better to limit what we say and be cautious not to say things in anger. That is great in principle, but it did not happen that day for me. God was still molding and shaping me, and at that particular stage in my development, I had a little more difficulty having what one might call an "unexpressed thought." I was boiling inside and could not hold my tongue. I turned around and faced the guy who made the comment and said something like this: "It's sad to me that a person pursuing the ministry as a pastor would be so stinking selfish. Just because you need to make a buck, you are going to rob those kids of the opportunity to have someone leading their ministry who actually loves them and is interested in their spiritual development. Somewhere out there is a guy or girl who would give everything they had for those kids as their kids' pastor, but you are willing to rob them of that just so you can pay some bills."

At first, I felt very righteous for telling them the truth; then I felt a little convicted for the way I delivered that truth; and then I felt awkward as we were all headed into the same Greek class. Oops!

My point is that this guy did not stand a chance in kids' ministry because his intention was to simply look for a job to pay the bills. And by the way, pursuing work is noble and necessary, but fulfilling the role of a children's leader as a staff person or volunteer requires a calling.

The calling is the anchor; it is the one thing that holds you steady during the storms of ministry life. It gets you through the rough patches you will experience in ministry. It also helps you to stay steady when your heart is broken by the reality that a very real enemy has unleashed hell on the kids of this world. It is the great paradox of oppression and enslavement. It looks different everywhere I go, yet it is the same. The kids in the affluent neighborhoods are enslaved to materialism, arrogance and self-centeredness; while the street kids of Manila and Rwanda are enslaved to extreme poverty, sex trading and emptiness. It looks very different, but it is still oppression and enslavement.

This is the very thing Jesus came to free us from. He came to free these kids from the sin of this world and give them a life of joy, contentment and purpose.

And you know who will be the ones to lead these children on behalf of Jesus? Those who are called.

Here are two questions for you: Why do you do what you do? Is your ministry just a job or is it a true calling?

2. The Compass Factor

Jesus knew three things that are extremely important if you want to make progress of any kind. He knew:

1. Where He was
2. Where He was going
3. How He would get there

Know Where You Are

To use a compass correctly you must first know where you are. As a teenager, I competed in a series of outdoor competitions that test your ability in a variety of camping and survival skills. One of these competitions included navigating our team through the mountains to a specific point on a map. I was designated the leader of the group, so I took the compass and map and led the charge. I knew how to use a compass and a map, and I was a risk taker. With that combination, I was confident that my group would be the first to arrive at the checkpoint and win the competition. I read the map correctly and utilized the compass correctly. However, what I failed to do was properly determine our starting point. To make a long story short, a search party had to come find us and transport my team to the checkpoint. Why did this happen? I did not correctly determine our starting point.

In order to have a ministry that is gospel-centered, you must first determine where you are. Here are a few ideas that might help in this quest:

Take time to reflect on . . .

- Your ministry direction
- Your schedule
- Your ministry environment
- Your community

Conduct an honest self-evaluation and then seek feedback and input from someone outside of your ministry environment.

Remember, you cannot get to where you want to go until you first know where you are.

Know Where You Are Going

Jesus had a very clear end goal in every situation. He knew what He wanted to accomplish. A gospel-centered children's ministry is one that knows the end goal. What is the end goal for the kids in your ministry? Typically, when I get in my car, I know exactly where I want to go. I have thought about it and I have a reason for going there. Our ministries should be given even more consideration. In what direction do you want your ministry to go?

Here are a couple of thoughts on knowing the direction of your ministry.

Pray for Guidance

I know this is one of those responses that we all know is the right thing to say, but I also know how easy it is to be busy with the Lord's work and not take the time to connect with the living God and gain the guidance we need.

Think About Possibilities

Okay, here is yet another obvious one: think. The reality is, many of us do not make "thinking time" a priority. Your brain is constantly at work, but how much of that is focused, concentrated thought, with the intent of finding solutions and innovations or discovering a new way to reach a generation that is in constant flux and motion?

In essence, this is getting your mind in gear to execute an action plan. But the action plan will not supernaturally appear on paper or your computer screen. You begin the process by thinking.

Make Sure You Are in Line with Your Senior Pastor's Vision

Do you know your senior pastor's vision for the church? Unfortunately, in many ministry settings, senior leadership is not always clear on the direction the church is going, so you may have to be proactive and ask the senior pastor to share that with you. It is imperative that your vision and the senior pastor's vision are headed in the same direction. If not, *you* will need to make the adjustment for the sake of the church. Two people cannot row a boat in opposite directions and expect to get anywhere.

Remember, if you do not know where you want to go, then it does not matter which path you choose, because any path will take you there.

Know How You Will Get There

This is your action plan that will take you from where you are to where you want to go. You might think of this as the coordinates on a map. You must use coordinates to plot your journey; otherwise, you will wander around aimlessly.

Jesus certainly had a plan of action. He knew exactly what He was trying to accomplish and what needed to happen in order to reach that objective. How about you? Do you know how you will move your ministry in the direction necessary to accomplish your goals?

A gospel-centered ministry has a plan in place to move it in the right direction. Here are several important components for you to consider as you develop your plan:

Your Curriculum

Never before have we, as children's ministry leaders, had so many options for curriculum. It is important to find the one that will accomplish the spiritual objectives you have set for a given ministry season. Do not be afraid to try a new curriculum or even use different ones for different series. With a little research, you can find the one that will best meet your ministry's current needs.

Your Environment

Your environment says a lot to your kids. The goal does not have to be to have the coolest facility in town, but you do want your environment to communicate to kids "you belong here."

Your Volunteers

You can do one of two things: (1) hope and pray that you have volunteers and they "get it," or (2) be strategic in bringing the right people around you and specifically training them to do their jobs. Recruiting volunteers always requires faith, but as you probably know by now, you must also have a plan to enlist and equip your volunteers.

Your Events

Big parties, water parks, lock-ins and a host of other events can all be an integral part of any children's ministry. The question is, how does the event play a part in the master plan for your children's ministry? Is there a specific purpose behind holding the event, or is it just another activity?

3. The Connection Factor

We can see in Jesus' ministry the importance of connection and the different types of connections. For example, Jesus was very selective in who He spent the bulk of His time with. Sure, He preached to thousands, but He chose a small group of people to do life with. Jesus knew what had to be accomplished. He knew the long-range plan, and that is what ultimately influenced His connections.

This is helpful to us in several ways. First, it is important to remember that we become like those we hang out with. This is both true for our kids and for us as adults. Maybe we are less impressionable as adults, but the principle is still valid.

Second, the Connection Factor is important because "iron sharpens iron" (Prov. 27:17). We learn from each other, we encourage each other, and we hold each other accountable. Who do you have in your life who "sharpens" you?

Third, the Connection Factor is evident in the fact that Jesus did not do ministry alone. Since Jesus did not do it alone, neither can we. Jesus was specific about those He recruited to be a part of His team. He was not willing to take any warm body just because He had to fill 12 slots before Sunday.

Jesus modeled for us the importance of connecting with others. We all need friends who will help us become our best. We also need connections with others in order to properly recruit and develop people to carry out the objective of sharing the good news.

4. The Choice Factor

When Jesus was on earth, He could not be in two places at once. He could not help everyone. Remember, He was both God and man. He walked this earth with a physical body that needed rest, nourishment, exercise and relationships.

Because He was man, even He could not do it all. Remember the story in which Jesus asked Peter to take Him across the lake away from the people? He did not want to go over there to do another big outreach; He was getting away from the people.

Here is a key point to remember in having a ministry that is gospel-centered: It is not hard to say yes to 10 good ideas. The real test of a leader is being able to discern the 3 best ideas and to be able to say no to 7 good ones.

The Choice Factor is about energy management. It is about knowing your limits, being aware of your load and knowing when to recharge. As human beings, we operate on a limited amount of energy. Of course, that energy can be replenished, but in order to do that, you must strengthen your realm of Choice.

You must be willing to make wise choices that include:

- How I spend my time
- What I read
- Who I hang out with
- Making time for recharging my batteries (knowing when to rest)
- How many Facebook and Twitter friends I follow

Setting Goals

One way to keep on the path of making the best choice in a world of unlimited choices and opportunities is to develop the discipline of goal setting. It helps to evaluate "What is most important?" or "What is the one thing I need to accomplish this season?"

Pretend with me that we are going on a road trip. Any time my family and I were going on a road trip, several things were predetermined, and other things were simply decided as we drove.

For example, here is what was predetermined:

- Where we were going
- How we were getting there
- What snacks we would have for the first leg of the trip (most important)

Here are a few things we would decide as we went along:

- What time we would eat
- Where we would eat
- What snacks we would pick up on the way

- Where we would refuel
- Did I mention where we would eat?

My point is this: There were a few components of the trip that did not require a predetermined plan. However, where we were going and how we were getting there were very important.

Goal setting helps us with the big picture in these ways:

- Predetermines the outcome
- Creates the pathway
- Provides measurable mile markers to ensure we are headed in the right direction

As you drive along in your car with a predetermined destination and the directions to get there, you need signs, mile markers or known landmarks to ensure you are headed in the right direction. Without the signs, mile markers or landmarks, it is difficult to know if you are going in the right direction.

I have driven a vehicle in several different countries and have come to the conclusion that hiring a driver is completely worth it. For example, in one country, there were very few road signs that gave any indication as to location. This made travel very stressful and difficult. This is the very thing that goal setting will help you overcome; it will help you know where you are going, how to get there, and if you veer off track.

What goals have you set for your ministry?

You cannot be everywhere at once and you cannot do every good thing that presents itself. You must choose how and where to spend your energy.

5. The Courage Factor

The Courage Factor is having the necessary faith for God to work and flow through you as you fulfill your calling.

Courage is not the absence of fear. It is the commitment to not let fear control you. As human beings, we are wired to take the path of least resistance. Many times, that causes us to lead very cautiously. And yes, given the fact that we work with kids, we must be extremely cautious, especially as it relates to the safety and security of our children. The courage I am referencing here is the willingness and determination to do the hard things in ministry.

Let me give you three examples. First, as courage relates to decision making. Rarely will you have all the data you need to make a proper decision. Many times, you will have to take a step of faith, an act of courage, and move forward with the information you have at the moment. The world moves too fast to have all the necessary information to make informed decisions. There is a difference between "waiting on God" and "delaying." Waiting on God is vital; but delaying because of fear can be crippling.

The second example has to do with confronting difficult people. As long as you are in ministry, you will have to deal with difficult people. One important lesson I have learned over the years is that the sooner you confront a difficult situation, the sooner the healing and transition process can begin. We tend to shy away from difficult people for multiple reasons. It may be because we have had a long friendship with the person; the person is close with the senior pastor; the person is a relative of a staff member or deacon; or maybe we just do not like confrontation. Whatever the reason, courage is necessary to move forward and do what needs to be done for the sake of the big picture.

The Courage Factor is also necessary as it pertains to taking risks. If fear controls you, you will spend all your mental energy finding a way not to fail. Failure is a part of life. It is one of the primary ways we learn. Of course, we all want to be seen as competent and capable leaders, but is it prudent to avoid risk taking just for the sake of self-preservation or reputation?

Unfortunately, some ministry settings do not encourage risk taking. Maybe you cannot take big risks, but I encourage you to venture out of the safety of routine to whatever degree you can. It is out there, on the limb, that you discover how far you can really go.

The Courage Factor helps you to discover things about yourself that you did not even know existed. God has innately entrusted you with so many incredible talents, gifts and passions that can be released with a simple act of courage.

6. The Creativity Factor

Jesus gave us incredible examples of creativity. Have you ever noticed that Jesus did not heal the same way two times in a row? Or that He communicated with people differently? Jesus was very aware of His surroundings and would use objects or the environment around Him to make a point. Jesus illustrates for us the power of being creative, whether He was communicating, healing or just hanging out.

To have a gospel-centered children's ministry, we must follow Jesus' example of creativity. Here are a few thoughts that might help.

Everyone Is Creative

Yes, that is what I said. Everyone is creative in some form. Maybe you cannot paint, but you can write. Maybe you cannot write, but you can plan. Maybe you cannot plan, but you know how to keep kids' attention. I have heard people say for years, "I'm just not creative." That is simply not true. You are creative. It is just that your form of creativity may not be connected to art, music or writing, which are the categories most often associated with creativity.

Creativity Is Work

There are times when we have these creative bursts or flashes of good ideas and thank God for them. But most of the time, we have to work at being creative. It means taking time to think, brainstorm and collaborate. It means having the courage to try new things and experiment. It means breaking out of our comfort zones.

To have a gospel-centered children's ministry, we must follow Jesus' lead of fostering creativity in our ministries.

7. The Commitment Factor

Is there a more beautiful and complete picture of commitment than the life of Jesus? From the beginning to the end, He displayed full-on commitment.

Because He was human, I am sure He had moments just like you and me: moments of frustration, fatigue, maybe even fear. He may have felt those natural human emotions, but those emotions did not control Him. Those God-given emotions exist for a reason, but they were never meant to be a driver in our life. The driver to keeping your life and ministry gospel-centered is commitment.

Think about when Jesus was arrested, beaten, mocked and tortured. What do you think was His greatest moment of anguish? At what point was Jesus most likely to throw in the towel? It was not due to the emotional pain. It was not due to the physical pain. The most crucial moment for Jesus, the moment He dreaded so badly that the Scripture says He sweated drops of blood, was that moment He took on the sins of the world and had to be separated from the presence of the Father.

This was a place Jesus had no reference for, no experience with and no way of knowing what the experience would be like. But what was certainly going into that moment was that He was committed! He was *all in*. His commitment eliminated the escape hatch. He knew what had to be done; and even in the most unrecognizable and unpredictable moment of His life, He was committed.

Let me now take on the role of a prophet. If you stay in children's ministry, you will face difficult circumstances. You will face troubled waters, deal with difficult people and experience unfair moments. The question is, when it happens, are you going to lean on the Commitment Factor and stay true to your calling (Calling Factor), or will you choose (Choice Factor) to turn and run?

Of course, there will always be transitions in your ministry; it is a natural part of life. I am certainly not proposing that you are uncommitted if you change ministries or churches. But it is all too easy to run from pain and run toward pleasure. It is a natural component of how we are constructed. That is all the more reason the Commitment Factor must be intact.

Just as we see in Jesus' ministry here on earth, there are multiple factors that contribute to the end goal of sharing the gospel—the good news. And while the seven factors we have explored in this chapter are not the only factors that contribute to a gospel-centered children's ministry, I do believe they are vital, and the implementation of these factors will continually point back to Jesus as the center of our ministry and leadership.

In a moment of honesty, think about what is really at the center of your ministry. What drives your decision making and your thinking, as well as the structure and tactics of your children's ministry? Is it drama, clowns, lights, props, puppets or great story telling? While all of these tools do contribute to the end goal, they cannot serve as the center of your ministry to children.

Our ministry to children is gospel-centered when our methodology, approach and structure point back to the central theme or objective of Scripture: sharing the good news; sharing Jesus Christ.

DISCUSSION QUESTIONS

1. What motivates you to stay faithful in children's ministry?
2. If you are called to do what you are doing, you will outlast the storms. What is a storm that you experienced but made it through in ministry?
3. You cannot get to where you want to go until you first know where you are. How well do you know your ministry direction?
4. As a ministry, are you in alignment with your senior pastor's vision? How can you do better at this?
5. The real test of a leader is being able to discern the best ideas and to be able to say no to the good ones. How do you do this?
6. To have a gospel-centered children's ministry, we must follow Jesus' lead of fostering creativity in our ministries. How can you encourage everyone in your ministry to be creative?
7. From the beginning to the end, Jesus displayed full-on commitment. How does this encourage you in your ministry?

5

Too Little for the Gospel?

JENNY FUNDERBURKE

Jenny Funderburke is the wife of Nate, her favorite computer geek, and mama to three crazy little girls: Kaylie, Brenna and Hallie. Jenny was born and raised in Chattanooga, Tennessee, where she came to know the Lord and was called into children's ministry. She graduated with a degree in elementary education from Samford University and received her master's degree from New Orleans Baptist Theological Seminary. After spending a decade of ministry in Alabama, Jenny now serves as the minister to children at West Bradenton Baptist Church in Bradenton, Florida. Her passion is to see the church reach families with the gospel, to make disciples around the world, and to see volunteers growing in what God has called them to do. Part of her heart lives in Belize, where she is passionate about ministry and mission work there.

Jenny also is a contributing editor for *KidzMatter Magazine* and helps coach Jim Wideman's Infuse leadership mentoring groups. She blogs about her random kidmin thoughts at jenny funderburke.com and can be found on Twitter as @jen_funderburke.

After Jesus and her family, Jenny's main loves are ice cream, Tennessee football and the beach.

When we think in terms of sharing the gospel and impacting children with the gospel, our thoughts go directly to tall kids. Of course, elementary-age children are the ones who are of age to begin responding and thoroughly understanding what Christ has done for them. However, the gospel is for everyone, and it can have an impact on children even before they reach the upper grades. We truly fail when we neglect the importance of the presence of the gospel within our youngest age classrooms.

The first six years of a child's life are the most crucial emotionally, socially, cognitively and, I believe, spiritually. The rest of the world is recognizing this fact. We live in the age of Baby Einstein, infant swim lessons and preschool computer classes. Our culture recognizes that little ones are like sponges. They absorb information at rates we can't understand. These younger years provide a brief window of opportunity that we too often neglect.

Recent brain research reveals that connections are created within a baby's brain that will last a lifetime. During the first three years, the brain grows and develops more than it ever will again. This is the process that God created for brain development.

As the church, it is time for us to recognize God's design and that our nursery and preschool classrooms exist for a greater purpose than babysitting and changing diapers. These environments serve as the very first experience children have with the gospel and have the potential to give them a solid foundation for faith.

Remember the preschool song "The Wise Man Built His House"? In Matthew 7:24-29, Jesus paints the picture of the difference between a solid foundation and a weak one. The house built upon the rock withstood the storm, while the house built on sand did not.

Foundations usually cannot be seen at first glance, but they are essential. In the same way, the work we do in the younger years in our children's ministry often feels unrewarding and unseen. It is easy to wonder if it even matters. However, just like in the story Jesus told, this foundation can make all the difference. Imagine a child who from his very first day in the church nursery is told that Jesus loves him. Imagine the foundation formed in a toddler as she learns that Jesus loves her even when she bites her friend. Imagine the foundation provided as a preschooler's mind is filled with the truths of the stories of Scripture. These are foundations built on a rock.

When we neglect the importance of the younger years, we run the risk of being like the foolish man. We don't want to build a foundation for faith solely upon the sand of "just baby-sitting," entertaining and goldfish crackers. One day, we want every child in our ministry to come to saving faith in Jesus Christ. We want each child to be a follower of Him and to be a world changer through the gospel. From the very beginning we must build on the rock of His Word. From babies through preschool age, our children deserve a solid foundation.

Can this foundation be laid later in life? Maybe. But Ephesians 5:16 reminds us of the importance of "making the most of every opportunity, because the days are evil." These opportunities for laying the foundation for the gospel begin in these early years.

The Gospel in the Nursery

I will never forget spending time with a friend when my firstborn was just six weeks old. I watched in amazement as my friend, who was holding her, stuck out her tongue and my baby proceeded to copy her. As a new mama, I realized right then that I was underestimating the capacity of what my little one was learning and understanding.

While the nursery will not be the place for gospel presentations and altar calls, it will be the place where key impressions are first made. The solid foundation begins here.

During this stage of life, children are developing their very first understanding of the world around them. In addition, a baby's very first understanding of what church is like and, potentially, who God is will be formed in the church nursery. This is far more than just baby-sitting. Their first impressions of who God is will come from the people who care for them in His name. While these impressions will primarily be formed by what parents do, church nursery workers are the next in line.

The primary emotional task babies must accomplish is to develop trust. This is why this ministry, at this life stage, is so very important. Trust is the very bottom line of the gospel! Before a child can ever learn to trust in Jesus, he or she must learn how to trust at all. In the book *Guiding Your Child Toward God,* author C. Sybil Waldrop points out, "Trust is born of dependency on the part of the baby whose needs are supplied upon demand with tender care by the one upon whom the baby depends. Thus, dependency and compassion combine to give birth to trust."[1]

So our first step in laying the foundation of the gospel for the babies in our care is to create an environment where a baby can learn to trust. What does this look like in the church nursery?

Train volunteers to respond quickly to babies' needs. Babies will not get spoiled in the hour or two that they are in your nursery. Train volunteers to lavish babies with love, attention and care. Change diapers quickly. Rock a few extra minutes. Make sure needs are met.

Over-staff your volunteers. In order to quickly meet babies' needs, make sure that you have more than enough help so that volunteers can be available to love on the babies.

Seek consistency. Trust is based on relationship. Consistency in the nursery is important. Having the same person with whom babies can build connection makes a whole lot of difference when that person tells them, "God loves you."

Emphasize nurture, not just baby-sitting. Encourage volunteers to take advantage of every moment they have with the babies. Their job is not to just contain the babies; their job is to use every opportunity to love them with the love of Jesus.

Combine care with the truth of God's Word. There should be a difference between the care provided by a secular daycare and the care provided in the church nursery. That difference should be the truth of the gospel—the good news of Jesus. When changing diapers, talk to the baby about how Jesus made him. As you rock the three-month-old, whisper to her about how much Jesus loves her. Remember, we have no idea how much babies are absorbing.

In addition to helping establish a little one's basic need of trust, a gospel-centered church nursery will also seek to infuse Jesus into every aspect of the environment. Again, this is working with the understanding that babies learn and understand so much more than we will ever know.

As already mentioned, talk to babies a lot. During diaper changes, while rocking, while playing or other times in the nursery room, you can tell a baby the following basic truths:

- Jesus loves you.
- God made you.
- God has a plan for you.
- You are precious to Jesus.

Dale Hudson, Director of Children's Ministry at Christ Fellowship Church, in Palm Beach, Florida, shares on his blog that his church's nursery has Bible promises hanging on the walls. Volunteers are instructed to pray these promises over the babies in their care. What an awesome and tangible reminder to both volunteers and parents that the nursery is about more than diapers!

Another valuable tool for creating a gospel-centered environment in your nursery is music. Music provides a calm background for your classrooms. Be intentional in finding music that worships Jesus and speaks Scripture. Cute and fun music is fine; but as you make the most of every opportunity with these little ones, seek lyrics that speak Jesus. Excellent resources include Yancy's "Roots for the Journey," "The Praise Baby Collection," and "Seeds Family Worship."

Above all, your greatest resources in building a nursery that points the tiniest ones toward Jesus are your volunteers. Do not settle for warm bodies in classrooms. Fill your nursery with people who get it. Find and train volunteers who are passionate about babies, but who are even more passionate about Jesus. Share with them the vision of laying the foundation for the gospel in these early years. Help them grasp the bigger picture of what they are doing. Then set them loose.

One of my all-time favorite nursery volunteers is a lady who overflows with the love of Jesus. I remember once how I foolishly wondered if we were best utilizing her passions by having her serve in the baby nursery. Then I discovered that she did not change a diaper without praying over that baby. The babies in her classroom were not just cared for; they were exposed to Jesus over and over again. That is the type of volunteer every baby deserves. That is the kind of volunteer who can revolutionize your nursery ministry.

Nursery ministry that focuses on the gospel requires quite a bit of faith. It is unlikely that you will see immediate evidences of the foundation you provide. Eight-month-olds are not going to head out to the mission field, nor are three-month-olds going to quote the "Romans Road to Salvation." But Hebrews 11:1 reminds us that "faith is confidence in what we hope for and assurance about what we do not see." Through faith we can be confident that God is planting seeds of the gospel in the hearts of babies. Through faith we can be assured that we are making a significant difference that we cannot see as we help babies establish a trust that will one day, Lord willing, be a trust in Jesus Christ as their Savior.

The Gospel and Toddlers

The stage of toddlerhood is amazing. Toddlers begin to repeat everything you say, like little parrots. They are funny and cute and continuously amaze all who are around them. Everything is an adventure. Everything requires exploration. Life is one discovery after another.

This stage is also amazingly frustrating. No longer are they the sweet infants who coo and giggle. As toddlers' independence grows, so does their stubbornness. And then they learn the word "no."

In this age group, children can now begin to interact with the gospel in their own age-appropriate ways. While the gospel is essential in the nursery, the children are passive in regard to it. The adults play the role of sharing and teaching while the little ones are not old enough to respond. The toddler stage is the first opportunity for children to learn truths about the gospel and begin to have an active role in the conversation.

That's because, let's face it, everything a toddler does is active! Including the gospel message in the toddler ministry environment does not involve much sitting still. If that is your goal, you are going to be very disappointed. In the toddler classroom, we share the same types of truths that we whisper into babies' sleepy ears. God loves you. God made you. God made everything. Jesus died for you. However, we share these in the midst of play and exploration.

As children play with animal toys, we are on the floor with them, sharing that God made every animal, and God made them. As they create with blocks, we repeat that God created them as well. Again, the goal is to make the most of every opportunity. Watching for teachable moments, we share the truths of the gospel as we go.

Those teachable moments often appear in some of the toughest moments. As soon as that word "no" comes out of a little one's mouth, it is a whole new ballgame. In this age group, children begin to actively choose to disobey and parents begin to cringe. Parents begin to develop their approach to discipline.

As kids this age begin to test the limits and disobey on purpose, this is an opportunity for the gospel to be lived out in your classroom. You can explain that what they did was wrong, but you still love them and forgive them. As a teachable moment, remind them that we all mess up, and that is called sin. Jesus still loves us, and He wants us to say "I'm sorry." This is the gospel.

In early years of discipline it is easy to default to "God loves you when you share with your friend" or "It makes God very sad when you hit your friend." Be very cautious with this type of wording. As kids get older, we don't want them to question, "If God loves me when I'm good, does that mean He doesn't love me when I'm bad?" In these simple, teachable moments, we want to communicate that sin is bad, but that is why Jesus came for us.

As communication skills grow, toddlers can begin to learn very simple memory verses. Will they comprehend every word? Probably not. But just as they begin to learn the alphabet song and sing the names of letters before they understand the critical role that letters have in language, so too they can begin to internalize the truths of Scripture. Meaning and theology can come later, and that is okay. But, again, you are laying a foundation in all communication.

When selecting verses, use a few simple criteria. Choose a verse that communicates a big truth. Choose simple words. Keep it short. Three to five words allow the most success for your little one. Also, remember to keep memorization fun. You can't sit a two-year-old down and drill him. Make it a game, or add motions. Work on remembering verses as you play or eat or do some other activity.

I remember doing this with our toddler many years ago, and I asked my husband, "Should we make sure she knows the book and verse number?" He was sweet enough not to laugh out loud. "Jenny, she's two. I think the words of the verses are most important." Of course, he was right. The point in all of this is not to get legalistic or create a list of to-dos that we have to do the right way. The purpose is to begin to plant eternal truth into small hearts.

Here are a few examples of verses that even young toddlers can begin repeating as their verbal skills grow:

- I will always praise you (Ps. 52:9).
- God is love (1 John 4:16).
- Jesus is alive (Matt. 28:6, paraphrase).
- Trust in the Lord forever (Isa. 26:4).
- Jesus said, "Don't be afraid" (Matt. 28:10, *NLT*).
- Be kind to one another (Eph. 4:32, *ESV*).
- God will help me (Isa. 50:7, *NKJV*).
- Worship the LORD (Ps. 96:9).

The Gospel and Preschoolers

Filled with wonder. Imaginative. Larger than life. Active. Curious. All of these words describe the world of preschoolers. Three- and four-year-olds are captivated by story. Pirates, princesses, adventure, mystery, the supernatural . . . all of these elements and more fill the minds of little ones. What better story for them to fall in love with than the story of the gospel?

It is through this avenue of story that preschoolers can grasp the basics of the good news of Jesus: God made us. People sinned. Jesus died for us. Jesus rose again. We can trust in Him.

These are the same basics we have whispered into the ears of newborns and helped toddlers learn to repeat. How do we now take these basics to the next level in the hearts and minds of preschoolers? There are four factors that should be present in your ministry to help the gospel stick.

Fully engage the story. As already mentioned, preschoolers thrive on story. There is a reason they love books and movies and television shows. There is a reason they tell you long-winded tales that may or may not have happened.

God has blessed us with His Word full of stories that point us toward His love and teach us of His truth. Don't let these become lifeless words in a teacher's book. Help the stories come alive. Help children fall in love with the stories of God so that they can begin to learn the truths of God. If they can realize at this age that there is power and wonder and awe in the pages of Scripture, they will be much more likely to remain connected to the Bible later in life. Use their imaginations. Use their sense of wonder. Help them see Jesus and what He has done for them.

Probably the best example of how this is done well for this age group is *The Jesus Storybook Bible* written by Sally Lloyd-Jones. This beautiful story Bible ties Jesus into every lesson, using imaginative and engaging language. The book repeatedly refers to the gospel as God's great rescue plan. It is very difficult to read through these stories and not get engaged in the truth of who He is.

Allow children to experience Him. Learning in the preschool environment cannot be passive. Teach the stories in a way that will be memorable. Involve the children. Encourage them to baa like sheep or swing a slingshot like David. Allow them to engage in the Bible stories physically and emotionally. Don't just have them sit and listen to the story; allow them to experience it. A child who can fully engage in a story is much more likely to experience the One the story is about.

Preschoolers are not too young to worship. Music is a powerful force in the heart of a child. Introduce music that teaches gospel truth and that glorifies Jesus. Give kids opportunity to worship Him through song, motions and dancing.

Repeat, repeat, repeat. While the learning capacity of this age group is huge, recognize that kids will best retain what is repeated. Keep the core truths of the gospel in the forefront of your teaching. Come back to them over and over again. Create simple wording that kids can easily repeat and remember. Just when you are sick to death of saying something, the three-year-old next to you probably just heard it for the first time. Help concepts stick by repeating them until you are tired of them. And then repeat them again.

Focus on others. Preschoolers are naturally egocentric. Their worlds revolve around themselves and they only see life through their own perspective. While this is a totally normal part of development, it is also crucial that this tendency be tempered. This is a wonderful time to help kids think outside of themselves by serving others in specific ways, learning about other people in other places, and looking to meet the needs of others. Providing opportunities for families to serve with their young children opens the door for kids to begin to learn that God's good news includes them but also goes far beyond them.

How Much Is Too Much?

One concern that preschool volunteers often have is knowing what the line is of how much to share, particularly concerning the story of Jesus' crucifixion and resurrection. There is often a fear of scaring a child or sharing too much too soon. No one wants a child to go home and have nightmares! Unfortunately, that fear sometimes leads us to leave out key components of the gospel, assuming that kids will get those parts when they are older.

The basics of the gospel cannot change or be neglected. Some parts of the gospel are hard to talk about with little people. Elements like the cross are graphic. There are no easy answers to the why questions. Sometimes it seems easier to skip over parts out of fear of how the kids will react. The gospel must be the whole gospel, even if you are teaching three-year-olds. I don't believe that leaving out the cross or other key ideas that feel uncomfortable should be an option.

Every detail is not necessary right now. Small kids do not need every gory detail. Saying that "Jesus died" or "Jesus died on the cross" is enough. Kids may not totally get how bad that was, and that is okay. How bad it was is not necessarily the most important point for a four-year-old. Rather, she needs to know that Jesus died for her because He loves her. That is enough.

Keep age-appropriateness in mind. A four-year-old can understand more than a three-year-old. A five-year-old can handle more detail than a four-year-old. Share the basics of the gospel in the child's language and with his or her level of development in mind.

Know your kids. Different kids can handle different levels of information. When sharing with a group, err on the side of caution and remember the most sensitive child in the room. When dealing with individuals, use discernment to know the appropriate level of detail for his or her maturity level.

Always point back to the good. Especially with this age group, we always want to remind them that the sad and the scary is not the end. Jesus is alive! He did not stay dead. Don't save that part for next week. Always share the rest of the story.

Answering Tough Questions

Have you ever felt like you would be very, very rich if you had a quarter for every why question you ever received from a preschooler? Wow, it is amazing the number of questions they can come up with! Questions can be scary because we are afraid of messing up or telling them the wrong thing. I often joke that neither my education degree nor my seminary degree prepared me for the theological questions my children come up with.

But questions really and truly are a good thing. Preschoolers process their world through the whys.

First, always be honest. It can be tempting to give safe, fluffy answers to little ones, even if the answers may not be totally true. Remember, the gospel is based on trust; and little ones' trust begins with us. Speak the truth, even if it probably will result in more why questions.

Second, always point back to Scripture. As best as you can, answer questions with God's Word. Remind children of what Scripture says and how that relates to their questions.

Third, answer based on the children's maturity. Don't answer more than they are asking or more than they are ready for. It is even okay to say, "That is something we can talk about more when you are older" or "This will make more sense later on." Don't avoid the question, but only give as much of an answer as their little brains can handle.

Fourth, remember that "I don't know" is a perfectly acceptable answer. There will be questions that either don't have an answer or that you don't know the answer to. It is okay to say "I don't know." If it is something that is unknowable, share with them that God did not tell us that in the Bible, so we can't really know for sure. If it is something you just don't know, offer to research it and come back with an answer. Who knows, you might grow too!

The bottom line is that questions should be seen as great opportunities for kids to continue to process the truths of the gospel on their terms. Grin, sigh and keep answering those millions of whys.

"Mama, I Wanna Be Bathtized"

My middle child is five years old. For the past year, she has been very focused on wanting to get "bathtized." The reasons have varied. Once it was because she was really hungry in church when the Lord's Supper was being served. Once it was because she really wanted to get in that water. The most touching time was following the death of a young friend, and she wanted to see him in heaven.

All of this was sweet, but her understanding of the gospel was still very much on a four-year-old level. She really, really loves Jesus, but she also really feels that you have to do lots of good things to go to heaven.

When we, as the church and as the family, do our job well, we should not be surprised when four- and five-year-olds who have heard the gospel message since infancy want to be baptized at a young age. Our challenge comes in walking the balance of encouraging their young faith while discerning what they are truly ready for.

First, fully engage the family in the conversation. Parents often get really nervous when their preschooler starts asking these types of questions. Mostly, they are afraid of messing up. When kids are in class and talk about "asking Jesus into my heart" or getting baptized, use that as an opportunity to talk to and coach parents.

Second, encourage the steps they are taking with Jesus. Can a four-year-old truly understand and accept the gospel? It probably depends on the four-year-old. Jesus talks an awful lot about the faith of a child, so I think we must be extremely careful in disregarding faith because of age. Many four-year-olds have a capacity for faith that could put many adults to shame. And some really do love Jesus, but all the pieces don't make sense yet. That's okay too. At this age, encourage and applaud children's love for Jesus wherever they are in the process. Don't doubt. Avoid discouragement. Any step they are taking toward Him is a good thing.

Third, discourage decisions based on fear. This could be the child's fear of not going to heaven or the parent's fear that something will happen to the child before he or she is baptized.

Fourth, encourage families to wait a bit for baptism or other public declarations of faith. I usually encourage families to wait until at least early elementary school before allowing a child to be baptized. This is not about doubting the child's faith; it is to give the child time to truly understand. Baptism has so much symbolic meaning that I believe it is to the long-term benefit of the child's faith to be able to understand as much of the meaning as possible. And we want kids to remember the event, which is much more difficult to do when it occurs in the preschool years.

Remind kids that baptism is not the most important thing. The most important thing is trusting in Jesus as Savior and loving Him more and more. Baptism just shows everyone else that you do. It still will be tough for kids to wait; but help them keep it in proper perspective. Talk a lot about the whys of baptism.

Partner with and Equip Parents

I cannot end this chapter without addressing one final component in nursery and preschool ministry that is essential in creating a gospel-centered environment. We have all seen the stats of the importance of engaging parents and how their impact on their children is far greater than what we can do in an hour or two a week at church.

Our babies, toddlers and preschoolers have a much better chance of growing up passionate about the gospel if they live in homes that are passionate about the gospel. But as you well know, this is not the default of most homes. It is easy to pass this burden on in our minds to the adult ministry of the church, but it is likely that with many of these new parents, the preschool ministry has more influence than we realize.

I believe these early years are a crucial timeframe in which we can capture parents. Generally, new parents are in a place where they know they need help. They don't have it all figured out yet. Often, God uses this life stage to bring parents back to Him as they realize they now have a new little life they are responsible for. They want to get it right.

Let's look at a few ways that we can engage parents:

- First, be a safe place. New mamas struggle with lots of mama guilt. They know they don't get it right, and even the old lady at Walmart will point out something they should do differently. Let your ministry be a place that is welcoming and nonjudgmental. Let parents enter and leave your environments feeling empowered to be a gospel-filled home, not discouraged that they will never measure up. Set parents up for a win rather than casting a vision for the "perfect" Christian home that may never be a reality.

- Second, provide resources. With each passing year, kids become more independent and parents tend to become less involved in the details of what their children are doing. New parents want to know how many dirty diapers their baby had and how many times they smiled. Toddler and preschool parents want to know what their child learned and how to reinforce that at home. Parents of fifth-graders generally just want them to be alive when they come back. Take advantage of this time of heavy involvement by providing resources as much as you can. Share what children are doing in class, but also share tips and methods for parents to incorporate the gospel into their everyday home life.

- Third, connect them to community that points them toward the gospel. Parenting young children can be a very lonely time. Help parents connect with each other through playgroups, small groups, topical Bible study groups, parenting classes, and the like. Make sure, though, that the community has a bigger purpose than just hanging out. Use these connection points as opportunities to further give parents age-appropriate resources to share the gospel within their home.

Yes, the preschool and nursery areas have lots of diapers, sippy cups, goldfish crackers, crying and bodily fluids. But we miss out when this is all we let it be. Allow your ministry to be a foundation-building, gospel-centered, Jesus-filled place, and watch God do big things now and in the future.

DISCUSSION QUESTIONS

1. On a scale of 1 to 10, how present is the gospel in your nursery and preschool ministry?
2. Of babies, toddlers and preschoolers, in which area do you feel Jesus is shared the most? What are some examples?
3. In each of these areas, where do you think your ministry can improve in being gospel-focused?
4. What do you think are the top three reasons why it is easy to neglect the gospel in these areas?
5. What would you communicate to volunteers in these areas as the top three reasons to increase a focus on the gospel?
6. What do children of each age group really need to know? Work together to create a list of basic gospel truths that should be shared with each age group. How can you make sure these are implemented in each age group?
7. What is your church's procedure if a preschooler expresses an interest in making a public decision for Christ? How will you walk through this with the family and the child?
8. How does your ministry coach parents in raising little ones to understand the gospel? What are some ways that you can connect with parents to help coach them?

Note
1. C. Sybil Waldrop, *Guiding Your Child Toward God* (Nashville, TN: B & H Publishing, 1991), p. 40.

6

A Ready Defense

KEN HAM

Reprinted from *Already Gone: Why Your Kids Will Quit Church and What You Can Do to Stop It* by Ken Ham, et al., ninth printing, (May 2012); pp. 95–116. Used with permission from the publisher (Master Books—www.nlpg.com).

The president, CEO and founder of Answers in Genesis—U.S. and the highly acclaimed Creation Museum, Ken Ham is one of the most in-demand Christian speakers in North America. Ham, a native Australian now residing near Cincinnati, Ohio, is the author of numerous books on the book of Genesis, the accuracy and authority of the Bible, dinosaurs, and the destructive fruits of evolutionary thinking. He appears frequently on American TV (in one year alone: Fox's *The O'Reilly Factor* and *Fox and Friends in the Morning;* CNN's *The Situation Room with Wolf Blitzer;* ABC's *Good Morning America;* BBC radio/TV, and more).

Ken hosts the daily radio program, "Answers . . . with Ken Ham," heard on more than 800 stations in America (and dozens more overseas) and is one of the editors and contributing authors for AiG's *Answers* magazine (a biblical worldview publication with over 70,000 worldwide subscribers). The high-tech Creation Museum near the Cincinnati Airport—which attracted 719,206 visitors (and several of the world's major media) in its first two years of operation—was Ken's brainchild.

Ken and his wife, Mally, reside in the Cincinnati area. They have five children and nine grandchildren.

But in your hearts revere Christ as Lord. Always be prepared
to give an answer to everyone who asks you to give the reason for
the hope that you have. But do this with gentleness and respect.
1 PETER 3:15

Susan is in fifth grade, and she loves it. Typical of children her age, her learning curve seems to be going straight up. She loves making friends; she loves reading books; she loves her mom and dad (though she's not sure about her big brothers that pick on her); and she loves Jesus . . . sort of. In all honesty, she's not too sure about Jesus right now. Yes, Susan grew up in the church and faithfully attended with her family on a regular basis. For the last several years she has enjoyed the bliss of faith as a child. Now, however, on the verge of adolescence, she is beginning to make her faith her own . . . or not. Her spiritual life is hanging in the balance, and no one even knows that's the case.

On Monday morning, with a ponytail sticking out from the side of her head and her favorite cartoon character embossed on her backpack, Susan will go to school.

At school, Susan learns many things. She learns about history, mathematics, language and science—both observational and historical science. She learns the science from men and women who wear white coats and safety glasses. They use test tubes and Bunsen burners. They dissect animals and use microscopes to look at cells, and they carry clipboards under their arms to record all of their scientific findings. To Susan, they look smart. They do research. They test hypotheses. They prove them with their experiments.

Susan knows that these people deal with real things—things that you can touch and feel—the kinds of things that matter. She spends many hours each week learning from these people. And she sees that they are dealing with fact. Because of this, when the same people talk about the history of the universe, dinosaurs, fossils, the origin of life and the like, and interpret them in a particular way (e.g., millions of years and evolution)—Susan thinks they are speaking with the same authority as when they discuss their observational science that involves what you can observe and experiment with directly. Susan can't discern the difference between observational and historical (origins) science; to her, it is all science. And that is how it is usually presented anyway.

On Sunday morning, Susan's mom and dad will dress her up and take her to church. For two hours or so, she will enjoy the company of friends under the care of committed Christian volunteers. To Susan, they look nice. They read stories to her. She is not sure if they are true or not—but they are nice stories. They don't really connect to reality, and they come from an old book anyway. They help her with her crafts. They sing songs together. Susan knows that these are good people and that they are teaching her about things that can't be seen. They tell her what to believe about many things. She actually has a 90 percent chance that her pastor and teachers will tell her that God created everything.[1]

However, there is a very strong likelihood she will get the idea she can believe in millions of years. Yes, this is a Bible-believing church after all. Or they will tell her *what* the Bible says, but they don't tell her *why* to believe. No charts, no timelines, no experiments. She's learning about things that she can't touch or feel, and she's not entirely sure anymore that these things really matter. All in all, Susan will get about 10 minutes of focused, spiritual input from adults this week at church, and none of it will include science. And she knows that they are dealing with faith.

Over the next few years, Susan's "worldview" (her philosophy of life) will be formed. She doesn't even know this is happening, but connections and assumptions are being made in her mind that will determine how she interprets everything that goes on around her for the rest of her life. By ninth grade or so, she will be able to articulate her worldview to herself and others. She will even think she came up with her worldview herself, but that's not true. Her belief has mostly been shaped by all of the input that she has been getting throughout her childhood. What has she learned? She has learned about the facts that supposedly govern the world, and she has learned about the faith that supposedly governs the heavens. The problem is that many of the "facts" that she has learned seem to contradict her faith—but no one talks about those things at church.

In her mind, there are obvious questions that no one seems to be asking:

- Why is there death and suffering if God is a good God?
- Why can't people of the same sex who love each other get married?
- Isn't it better to get divorced than live unhappily?
- How can the earth be only a few thousand years old when it "looks" so old?
- Why is Jesus the "only way"?
- How come dinosaurs have nothing to do with the Bible or church?

Because no one asks these questions, she assumes that no one has the answers to these questions. She realizes that church people seem to have faith in spite of the "facts" that she has been told. That didn't matter so much as a child, but now on the edge of adulthood, she begins to feel the disconnect: *The facts are relevant; faith is not. If you want to learn something that's real, important and meaningful, you do that at school. If you want to learn something that is lofty and emotional, you do that at church. At school, they teach about everything—fossils, dinosaurs, marriage (different views, gay marriage, and so on), sex, the origin of life, what is "right" and "wrong," different religions—they learn about everything!*

Yes, she's still in elementary school, but she is on her way to being one of the 20-somethings who will leave the church and never come back—not even during the holidays; not even when she has children of her own. She's not cynical, just skeptical. She's not uncommitted, just indifferent. She will become what George Barna calls "the Invisible Generation" that brashly challenges us to respond to her honest questions:

All I want is reality. Show me God. Tell me what He is really like. Help me to understand why life is the way it is and how I can experience it more fully and with greater joy. I don't want empty promises. I want the real thing. And I'll go wherever I find that truth system. —Lisa Baker, age 20[2]

Susan is already sliding down the slope of unbelief. She's *willing* to believe in something that is real, but no one offers her anything like that on Sunday morning. They tell her *what* to believe, but they do not tell her *why*.

No one talks about it at home either. By and large, what she is taught at secular school is not dealt with. She is given no answers. Even at Christian school, the textbooks don't really teach answers to the skeptical questions of the day. And even in most homeschools, kids may be taught the Bible is true, but many don't understand how a non-Christian thinks, nor are they prepared to answer the questions of the day. In many instances, the same compromises with or indifference about millions of years and evolution are no different than the compromising churches. In the vacuum of answers, her doubts begin to solidify.

When did Susan's problems start? Did they start with television? Did they start with secular school? Did they start in Sunday School? Actually, her problems started a long, long time ago . . . a long time ago in a garden.

Defenseless

Adam and Eve had it made. In fact, I don't even think we can imagine the beauty, the harmony and the intimacy that they shared with each other, with the world and with God. It was all "very good," as God proclaimed. In unhindered exploration of God's creation, they walked freely in the Garden of Eden, "naked and unashamed," without fear, without condemnation, without threat. Yes, it was very good, but it didn't last. God placed only one parameter on Adam and Eve: "of the tree of the knowledge of good and evil you shall not eat, for in the day that you eat of it you shall surely die" (Gen. 2:17).

The serpent in the garden was more sly than anything else that God had made. Having rebelled against God and having been thrown down from heaven, Satan laid down the doubt that would lead to the sin that would distort, decay and bring death to the perfection that God had created. It was a simple and subtle scheme. It wasn't a direct accusation at first—just a hint of a suggestion. It was the beginning of doubt—the same doubt that plagues the generation that is now exiting the Church. Satan simply brought up a slight possibility:

> Did God *really* say, "You must not eat from any tree in the garden? . . . You will not surely die" (Gen. 3:1-4, emphasis added).

Did God really say . . . ? It was the first attack on the Word of God. Since then, the attack has always been on the Word of God. The attack manifests itself in different ways during different areas of history. But the question is really always the same: *Did God really say . . . ?* Throughout the centuries, Satan has attacked the Word of God and attacked the human soul by casting doubt into the truthfulness of what God has said and the relevance of God's words in practical everyday life. In the last 100 years, the attacks have begun to sound more and more scientific:

- Did God really say that He created everything? Surely science has proven that the big bang happened spontaneously, without any outside force.
- Did God really say that He created the earth in six days? Surely science has proven that life evolved over millions and billions of years.

- Did God really say that He created life? Surely science has proven that the right chemicals in the right place over a long enough period of time will spontaneously generate living forms.
- Did God really say that He created humanity? Surely science has proven that the human race is really just a highly evolved life form that is the product of time and random chance.
- Did God really send a worldwide Flood in the time of Noah? Surely science has shown there never was a global Flood, and that the fossil layers were laid down over millions of years—not by a Flood.

The youth of today are wrestling with such questions. Fact seems to disprove faith. The church in England responded to this attack by doing almost nothing. Actually, they did do something—they basically agreed one could accept the teachings of the world concerning the past, and reinterpret the Bible's account in Genesis. It focused on issues of faith and left its people defenseless against the so-called facts. To a certain extent, evangelical Christianity has done the same thing in America. Oh, yes, there are a few people in every congregation who seem to specialize in "apologetics." They are the brainiacs who read and study and seem to have a quick answer for everything. But they are few and far between. The rest of us try to ignore our doubts, leave the intellectual battles to someone else and just focus on Jesus and the gospel.

But in this day and age, we must see that an attack on the Word of God is an attack on the gospel. Without the Word of God, we have no gospel. Without the Word of God, we have no morality. Without the Word of God, we have no record of our past and no prophecy for our future. Without the Word of God, Christianity cannot stand.

Biblical Authority Issues

Those of us who are born-again Christians believe that Jesus Christ bodily rose from the dead. After all, as Paul states in 1 Corinthians 15:14, (*NASB*): "And if Christ has not been raised, then our preaching is vain, your faith also is vain." We believe as real historical fact that Jesus Christ bodily rose from the dead.

But let me ask you a question: How do you know Jesus Christ rose from the dead? You were not there, and you don't have a movie rerun, so how do you know? Because the Bible says, that's how. We accept that the Bible is the revealed Word of God—it is inerrant, inspired, the "God-breathed" revelation from our Creator. And as such, we let God's word speak to us through this written Word. If it is history, we take it as history. We don't try to force our ideas onto God's Word; we let it speak to us in the language and context in which it is written. How about Jesus actually walking on water? Or that Jesus fed thousands of people from just a few loaves and fishes? Or that Jonah was swallowed by a great fish? We know, because it's in the Bible.

But if I go to many churches in America and ask if God created everything in six ordinary days; if death of animals and man came after sin; if there was a worldwide Flood in the time of Noah; and so on, I suddenly get responses like, "Well, we wouldn't say that. The days could be millions of years. God could have used evolution. Noah's Flood might have been a local event or really didn't have much impact on the earth," and all sorts of similar statements.

Now, I want you to understand what has happened—this is key to understanding what has happened to our culture, and key to understanding why our kids are leaving the Church. This is the crux of the issue. It is an issue of authority—biblical authority.

It is true that the literal events of Genesis are foundational to all doctrine—to the gospel. In Matthew 19:4-7, when Jesus was explaining the doctrine of marriage, He quoted from the creation account of Adam and Eve to teach the doctrine of one man for one woman. The whole meaning of the gospel is dependent upon the account of the Fall of man, and thus original sin, as given in Genesis. Ultimately, every single biblical doctrine of theology, directly or indirectly, is founded in the historical account given in Genesis 1–11. And Genesis is written as typical historical narrative (not like the Psalms that are written as typical Hebrew poetry). If one undermines this history, or reinterprets it, or tries to claim it is myth or symbolic, then one undermines the foundation of the rest of the Bible, including the gospel.

But even given this, there is something far more crucial—it is the very WORD itself, the authority of the book we call the Bible.

The reason we know Jesus rose from the dead is that we take God's Word as written. The reason we know a fish swallowed a man is that we take God's Word as written. And if you take God's Word as written in Genesis (and it is written as history and quoted from as history throughout the Bible, as did Jesus Himself in His earthly ministry), it is very clear that God created in six ordinary days; that man and animals were vegetarian before sin; there was a global Flood; and there was an event after the Flood called the Tower of Babel that formed the different people groups.

Thus, one can't have a fossil record, of supposed millions of years before man, containing evidence of animals eating each other, bones with diseases like cancer and thorns said to be hundreds of millions of years old when everything was described by God as "very good" and animals and man were vegetarian and there was no sin and thus no death and disease or thorns before Adam's rebellion. The ultimate reason so many in the Church (including professors at Bible colleges, seminaries and Christian colleges) reinterpret the Genesis account of creation, or say it is not important, is because of the influence of the idea of millions of years and evolutionary teaching.

Here is the point. Stand back and consider the big picture. If we teach our children (or anyone) to take God's Word as written concerning the Resurrection, the miracles of Jesus, and the account of Jonah and the great fish that swallowed him, but then tell them we don't need to take Genesis as written but can reinterpret it on the basis of the world's teaching about millions of years and evolution—we have unlocked a door.

The door we've unlocked is the door to undermine biblical authority. We are really saying, "We want you to take God's Word as written according to literature and language in certain places—but not here at the beginning in Genesis." What we have actually done is made man the authority over God's Word. We have taught our children that they can take what they learn at school and can reinterpret the Bible's clear teaching in Genesis to supposedly fit this into the Bible. By staying silent and not defending Genesis, we are "teaching" our children that we don't have to take God's Word as written, and man can reinterpret God's Word according to what the majority in the culture might believe.

Scripture teaches that if there is sin or compromise in one generation, and it is not dealt with, it is usually observed to occur to a much greater extent in the next generation, and so on. When we unlock that door in Genesis, the next generation usually pushes that door open further—and then the next generation further again, and then the next further again—until eventually all of the Bible is rejected. There is a loss of biblical authority each generation until it becomes an epidemic throughout the Church and nation. The structure of Christianity (its morality, its Christian worldview) collapses, to be replaced by a man-centered structure where moral relativism would pervade the culture. That is what we have seen across Europe, and before our very eyes in America.

An Open Door

So why do we tolerate ideas that undermine the authority of God's Word? We think that simply because a secular humanist or an atheist is not directly attacking Jesus or the Cross that he's not attacking them at all. If the mass media and education systems directly targeted Jesus and the Resurrection, most in the Church would be up in arms. But if the foundation of those beliefs is attacked and weakened first (the attack on the Word itself), then unbelief creeps across the country and through the Church, slowly and surely, while we have to fight more and more for the things we value in our faith (e.g., the Ten Commandments, Nativity scenes and so on).

The world, the devil, and even our sinful human tendencies have caused a deep, dark shadow of doubt to fall across God's Word. *Did God really say . . . ?* In regard to the events in Genesis—six literal days, and so on—most people would say no, because the Word of God has been under successful attack. In Europe the attack began when scientists threw doubt on the age of the earth. In America today, those same attacks are shattering the foundation upon which the Church and the gospel depend. Actually, the Bible itself warns us that such attacks will happen, and we need to be ready for them. In 2 Corinthians 11:3 (*NASB*), Paul warns us that Satan will use the same attack on us that he did on Eve:

> But I am afraid that, as the serpent deceived Eve by his craftiness, your minds will be led astray from the simplicity and purity of devotion to Christ.

And what was the method used on Eve? *"Did God really say . . . ?"* He got Adam and Eve to doubt and thus disbelieve the Word of God. This attack was meant to cause Adam and Eve to reinterpret God's Word based on their own appraisal of things. They looked at the evidence—the beautiful fruit—and decided that God's Word couldn't mean what they thought it meant. It was okay to reinterpret it and determine truth for themselves. I call this "the Genesis 3 Attack"! Genesis 3 Attacks have occurred over and over again throughout history. And in this era (particularly since the late eighteenth century), the Genesis 3 Attack has manifested itself as science attempting to disprove the account of creation, the Flood and the Tower of Babel in Genesis. Our culture today is in great danger—the Genesis 3 Attack has hit the Church and the culture!

While I have very strong feelings about the direction that our culture is going, I do not believe that culture can be changed from the top down. Sure, you might get the laws changed for the next four years, but the next guy who gets voted in can erase everything. You might be able to win a few legal battles regarding freedom of speech, but before we know it, the next group will be telling us to sit down and shut up. Why? Because they don't believe the Book from which we speak. You see, the culture has changed from the foundation up, as reflected in the predominant secular worldview and relative morality. The culture went from being built on the foundation of God's Word to being built on the foundation of man's word. And this has also happened in the Church. When the Church adopted millions of years and evolutionary ideas into the Bible, they put man in authority over God's Word, making man the ultimate authority, not God! No wonder the kids are walking away from the Church!

At its heart, Answers in Genesis (AiG) is not a creation-versus-evolution ministry, and we're not out to change the culture. The Bible doesn't say to go into all the world and change the culture, but to go into all the world and preach the gospel. The culture changed because hearts and minds changed in regard to the Word of God. To change the culture back, hearts and minds need to be changed toward God and His Word. When such changed hearts and minds, committed to the Word of God, shine light and distribute "salt" in the culture—then the culture will change.

We see it as our job to defend the Christian faith, stand on the authority of God's Word without compromise and proclaim the gospel of Jesus Christ. And when the relevancy of the Word of God is restored, lives will be changed as the power and authority of the living Word of God empowers their lives. Then, we believe, these individuals will permeate the culture by living truthfully and honestly in harmony with godly principles . . . and *then* culture will be changed from the bottom up. That's what this ministry is all about. We strive to get information out there to change the foundation and worldview of individuals so the culture will naturally be changed from the heart.

Satan deceived by his craftiness, the Word of God was compromised and people's minds were corrupted from the simplicity of the gospel and Jesus.

But why should we be surprised? Psalm 11:3, (*NASB*) says, "If the foundations are destroyed, what can the righteous do?" Our foundation is the Word of God. We need to defend the Word of God as one of our top priorities as Christians. If we are to give a strategic and effective response to the wave of souls who are leaving the Church, these issues must be addressed.

The Attack Today

In 2009, AiG published the results of research conducted by America's Research Group in the book *Already Gone* (Green Forest, AR: Master Books, 2009), coauthored by Britt Beemer and myself. In our survey, we asked a thousand young adults who have left the Church if they believed that all the accounts and stories in the Bible are true and accurate. Of those, 44 percent said no, 38 percent said yes, and 18 percent didn't know. We asked those who said no this follow-up question: If you don't believe all the accounts and stories in the Bible are true and accurate, what made you begin to doubt the Bible?

- 24% It was written by men.
- 18% It was not translated correctly.
- 15% The Bible contradicts itself.
- 14% Science shows the world is old.
- 11% The Bible has errors.
- 7% There's so much suffering in the world.
- 4% Christians don't live by the Bible.
- 4% Evolution proves that the Bible is wrong.

Look at those results again. If you add up all of the responses related to biblical authority, you'll see that 82 percent of those who said they did not believe all the accounts and stories in the Bible are true and accurate did so because of doubts about the authority of the Bible. Then we asked this other question: Does the Bible contain errors?

Forty percent said yes and another 30 percent didn't know. Only 30 percent said that the Bible does not contain errors. Those who said the Bible does contain errors cited reasons such as alleged contradictions and disagreement between Genesis and evolutionary science.

These are the doubts that students like Susan are facing. These are the doubts that are plaguing the hearts of the next generation. For the group that will never come back to church and never comes on holidays, these issues are even more pronounced. It would seem logical then that if we are to strategically respond to the devastating epidemic of young adults who are leaving the evangelical Church, we should be addressing these issues. Responding to these attacks on our Bible should be at the forefront of our attempts to restore relevancy to the Word of God and make our churches relevant to this generation. It is so obvious that we need to be teaching apologetics in our churches—creation apologetics and general Bible apologetics! The fact that this is not happening in the majority of our churches, nor in the majority of Bible and Christian colleges and seminaries, is one of the great travesties of this age in regard to the Church.

What can we do to help youth who are struggling with doubts?

Resources for Reclaiming Biblical Relevance

Let's take another look at the situation that the first-century Apostles were facing and draw another parallel between their situation and ours today. Is a child like Susan growing up in Athens, or is she growing up in Jerusalem? In other words, is she growing up as a "Jew" in a society where biblical belief is assumed, or is she growing up in a "Greek" society that is secular and skeptical?

The answer is that Susan is actually doing a little of *both*. Part of her is growing up in a church that believes. Christianity is the accepted norm on Sunday morning. The problem is that the moment she steps out the door, she enters a world that is more like Athens. Because of that, Susan's church should be "equipping the saints for the work of the ministry" in an unbelieving world by teaching her and her church to defend the Word of God from the very first verse against the skeptical attacks of this age. Not only would this help protect Susan's faith from the attacks she gets in the world, but it would also arm her and the rest of her congregation to take the offensive. In both situations, the foundation of the authority of the Word of God both inside and outside the Church needs to be rebuilt.

The Church needs to be reminded over and over why the majority of students begin to doubt the Bible in middle and high school—and then *diligently* deal with the issues by introducing relevant apologetics courses (teaching a logical, reasoned defense of the faith) by at least middle school (even before).

As I travel around the world teaching on biblical apologetics, I find that whether my audience is primarily secular or Christian, regardless of what country I'm in, I get asked the same basic questions—such as (to name only some of them):

- How do you know the Bible is true?
- Hasn't science disproved the Bible?
- Isn't the world millions of years old?
- What about carbon dating?
- How did Noah get all the animals on the ark?
- But don't we observe evolution because we see animals change—we see bacteria become resistant to antibiotics?
- If God created Adam and Eve, only two people to start with, where did all the people come from?
- How come there are so many different "races" of people?
- But dinosaurs don't fit with the Bible; how do you explain them?
- Where is the evidence for a global Flood?
- How can you believe in a loving God when there is so much death and suffering around us?

Most Sunday School lessons, sermons, Bible studies and so on, are not teaching people how to answer the questions of the day. They are not connecting the Bible to the real world. They are not teaching people how to defend their faith—and we wonder why we are losing them. Not only is apologetics (a logical defense of the faith) not taught in most churches and Sunday Schools, it is not taught at most Bible colleges or seminaries—or it is actually taught against! Church leaders today seem to think that programs, entertainment, music and many other things are what we need to reach people and keep them in church.

However, our research also showed something very different—that people want good Bible teaching. It is the preaching of the Word and making it relevant to them in today's world that they need and want. But this is not happening even in Sunday School in the majority of instances, let alone the rest of the church programs.

The Bible is not some "pie in the sky" philosophical book. It's a real book that is really connected to the real world. It is a history book that connects to dirt, fossils, stones, bones, tsunamis, earthquakes, oceans, mountains, death and the like. It has *everything* to do with geography, biology, anthropology and sociology. The Word of God has never changed, but the Church's perception of the Word of God changed when it failed to engage the scientific community on matters of fact as well as faith. It's time to change that and be true to the challenge that Peter left for each of us to follow:

> But in your hearts revere Christ as Lord. Always be prepared to give an answer to everyone who asks you to give the reason for the hope that you have. But do this with gentleness and respect (1 Pet. 3:15).

Typical churches use materials that are more geared for "the Jew in Jerusalem" who has a developed religious background and lives in a religiously friendly society. That's just not the case anymore. Our society is now immersed in secularism. It's absolutely essential that we learn to defend the Bible and the Christian faith, for the sake of our faith and our children's faith and to evangelize a society that has a highly diminished understanding of biblical truth. I firmly believe that we are now in the era of the "Greeks" . . . yet our churches and Sunday Schools are still teaching us like "Jews." See the problem?

We do not have a ready defense in most of our churches—*yet*. But, thankfully, God has supplied us with all the weapons and shields we need to defend ourselves and to take the offensive in reclaiming the relevance of God's Word in our churches and in this society. Our defense must be strategic. As families and as a Church, we need to think through the threats that lurk around us and be willing to protect our families and our churches from the onslaught of ideas that continually cause us to question if God really said what He says He did.

I'm advocating a completely new approach to how we educate ourselves as Christians! God's Word and the Christian faith *are* supported/confirmed by the facts. The disconnect between faith and fact is nothing but an illusion created by an overwhelming misinterpretation of the facts. Good observational science *supports* faith. It always has and it always will. It's time to bring the facts back into our faith. Training yourself, your family and your church to be defenders of the faith is an exciting and empowering adventure. It can change the Church—it can change the world. It's time to attack doubt with courses and preaching and teaching that defend God's Word against the attacks of this age!

That sounds like a huge endeavor, and in some ways it is—in fact, it will take a *lifetime*!

The data from our survey showed that questions about Genesis represented about 40 percent of all the concerns. Ultimately, if we are unable to defend Genesis, we have allowed the enemy to attack our Christian faith and undermine the very first book of the Bible. We need to be able to defend our faith from general attacks *and* defend against the specific attacks on the Book of Genesis. The number of resources now available is wonderful.[3]

This Sunday, take a second look at the kids coming through the door of your church. Like Susan, most will appear to be excited, enthusiastic and engaged. The fact is, about 30 percent of them are kids who are beginning to wrestle with significant doubts about the relevancy of the Word of God. Overall, two-thirds of young people will walk away from the church because of their doubts about the truth of God's Word. What can we do to help children like her? What can we do to protect our own kids as well as our own hearts from the attacks on God's Word? By defending and teaching the Bible from the very first verse and then depending on God to keep us faithful to our call!

DISCUSSION QUESTIONS

1. What surprised you most about this chapter?
2. In the beginning of the chapter, we met Susan, a fifth-grader with lots of questions, including:

   - Why is there death and suffering if God is a good God?
   - Why can't people of the same sex who love each other get married?
   - Isn't it better to get divorced than live unhappily?
   - How can the earth be only a few thousand years old when it "looks" so old?
   - Why is Jesus the "only way"?
   - How come dinosaurs have nothing to do with the Bible or church?

   How well is your ministry doing to help kids find the answers to these questions?

3. How can you better equip the teachers and leaders in your church to not only tell kids what to believe, but why to believe it?
4. What questions are the kids in your church and community wrestling with?
5. In the chapter, Ken talks about changing culture from the ground up. He says that we must start with God's Word as our foundation. On a scale of 1-10, how well is your church's curriculum using God's Word to lay a solid foundation? Do you need to make any adjustments?
6. How has this chapter impacted your approach to ministry?

Notes
1. Only 10 percent of all the people in our survey, which again, attended conservative churches, said that their pastor said it was okay to believe in Darwinism.
2. George Barna, *The Invisible Generation: Baby Busters* (Barna Research Group, 1992).
3. I encourage you to visit AnswersBookstore.com, where you will find numerous resources that will help you teach your children solid, biblically based apologetics, including our new *Answers Bible Curriculum*.

7

Special Needs

MARIE KUCK

Marie is cofounder and executive director of Nathaniel's Hope, a growing national ministry dedicated to sharing hope, encouragement and practical assistance to kids with special needs (VIP Kids) and their families, as well as educating and equipping local churches to reach out and minister to these families. As an ordained minister, Marie has served as a youth minister on church staffs for over 10 years in Chicago, Minneapolis and Orlando before becoming a mom to Nathaniel, a child with multiple special needs.

At the age of four and a half, Nathaniel unexpectedly had a change of address from earth to heaven. Following the death of their son, who had brought them into the community of special needs, Marie and her husband, Tim, were compelled to steward these circumstances and responded to the call to birth Nathaniel's Hope in June 2002.

Nathaniel's Hope has developed many programs to assist VIP families and help people engage with those impacted by disability, including Buddy Break—a fast-growing national network of churches working together to provide free respite care to VIP kids. Nathaniel's Hope has equipped churches in 15 states to minister to VIP families, with the goal of partnering with 1,000 churches by 2020. Other programs include a "National VIP Birthday Club" and "Make 'm Smile," an annual community festival celebrating kids with all types of special needs. On June 2, 2012, Nathaniel's Hope hosted more than 15,000 people at their 10th Annual Make 'm Smile Festival in downtown Orlando, including nearly 2,000 VIP kids.

Marie, a graduate of Wheaton College, enjoys sharing her passion for VIP kids on national platforms, speaking and leading workshops at CPC, CM Leaders, D6 and various denominational conferences. Marie has taught in the Department of Communications at North Central University and cohosted "Today's Family," a local Christian television talk show in Orlando. Marie and Tim are cofounders of Teams Commission for Christ International (TCCI), a short-term missions organization equipping and sending short-term missions teams into Guatemala and El Salvador. Marie has served as producer of the "GO Prepared" short-term missions training series.

Marie currently serves on the board of Pine Castle Christian Academy in Orlando and considers herself to be a "mom on a mission." She and her husband, Tim, have been married for 23 years and have 3 children, Brianna (20), Ashley (18) and Nathaniel (4½, residing in heaven). The Kucks reside in Orlando, Florida.

www.NathanielsHope.org
MarieK@NathanielsHope.org

The words "special needs" had always intimidated me.

I didn't know how to connect with "those" kids. I wasn't trained in special education, nor did I ever really think that it was my job to get equipped. There were enough challenges trying to put together a vibrant ministry program that would engage the masses. Building the ministry was time consuming. I didn't really have extra discretionary time or resources to even consider ministry to kids with special needs.

I never really thought about who was ministering to "those" kids, nor did it ever occur to me that I could be the one or, even more sobering, *should* be the one to do something.

I was pretty out of touch with this community.

It never occurred to me that when Jesus said, "let the children come unto me," He meant *all* kids. Not just the ones who were easy to minister to, but *all* kids, which included kids like Meghan, who had Down syndrome and might require me to invest a little more effort in adapting my lesson plans; kids like Joey, who struggled with ADHD and had trouble focusing on what we were doing in the classroom; kids like Timmy, who needed extra assistance because of physical disabilities; or Maddie, who had autism and would stretch me to the limits because of extreme behavior issues and communication challenges.

To be honest, I just didn't know what I didn't know.

That all changed when God brought one of "those" kids into our life. His name was Nathaniel.

Nathaniel was born with multiple special needs and immediately thrust us into the world of disability. Unlike the addition of our other two children, with the addition of Nathaniel, our family's life was changed overnight as we were catapulted into this foreign world filled with unplanned hospital visits, long sleepless nights, social isolation, financial burdens, care that demanded 24/7 attention, and stress factors that were off the chart (two to three times higher than a typical family would experience). This was a different dream than the one we had anticipated for our son and young family. Balancing these new stresses while trying to maintain sanity raising a toddler and preschooler were not part of our scripted plans for life.

Welcome to the world of disability—a place where dreams are abruptly interrupted and weary parents find themselves fighting for everything . . . the healthcare system, insurance companies, the school system, and yes, even the church.

Something just didn't seem right.

Did God really love my child who was not perfect?

If so, why was it so hard for others to love him? Was he an accident? Or did God truly fearfully and wonderfully create Nathaniel and those other unique kids in His image?

What application did the gospel have for my imperfect child?

Did Jesus die on the cross for him, or did he get a special pass into heaven? How important was it for him to have the opportunity to learn about Jesus? Was the gospel for Nathaniel? Was there a place for him in the Body of Christ?

A place not just for Nathaniel, but for all of those other uniquely abled kids. In fact, the numbers are staggering. In the U.S. today, there are more than 50 million people with disabilities. Of that number, more than 20 million are kids or teens. National statistics would tell us that less that 10 percent of families impacted by disability attend church. Have we let them know that their uniquely abled kids are welcome?

What does the Bible have to say about welcoming kids with special needs? Actually, Jesus addresses this in Luke 14:12-14, *NASB*:

And He also went on to say to the one who had invited Him, "When you give a luncheon or a dinner, do not invite your friends or your brothers or your relatives or rich neighbors, otherwise they may also invite you in return and that will be your repayment. But when you give a reception, invite the poor, the crippled, the lame, the blind, and you will be blessed, since they do not have the means to repay you; for you will be repaid at the resurrection of the righteous."

Let me paraphrase this.

When you have church every Sunday, who is on your guest list? Don't just think about inviting the well-behaved kids, the ones who love Jesus and are easy to minister to . . . the kids on the honor roll, who score high stanines, or are above average with their talents and abilities . . . or well-behaved kids who will hang on every word you speak, or kids who come from well-to-do families. But when you gather together for Sunday School or your Wednesday night programs, be sure to invite the Meghans, the Joeys, the Timmys and the Maddies . . . kids who might have some special needs . . . who may be a little harder to teach, who may challenge you to work a bit harder or take you way out of your comfort zone . . . but these are the kids who need to be on your VIP list! When you do this, you're going to be blessed big time!

Does your guest list include kids with special needs? One out of 10 kids under the age of 14 have some type of disability.

Are they coming to your weekly celebration?

Have you extended an invitation? These kids were VIPs to Jesus!

Did you know that 70 percent of the miracles that Jesus performed were to the disabled community? I think the disabled community was close to His heart. In fact, I think that if Jesus were physically with us on Sunday morning, He would be the first to volunteer to minister to kids with special needs—VIP kids! I would suggest that not only does Jesus propose welcoming them in, but He would want us to be deliberate and intentional in doing so!

What does it mean to be intentional?

Being intentional means that every time you open the doors of your church, you are making a special place at your table for kids with special needs. Rather than scrambling to find a place for them when they show up at your door, you have anticipated their arrival and have a plan to receive them. Even if you don't have it all figured out because of the uniqueness of every child, you let the parents know that together you will find a way for their VIP to belong. In fact, you may even put out an invitation on your website, in your church bulletin, have clearly labeled parking spots for special needs families, or even an announcement in the community letting families know that these VIP kids are welcome at your gatherings. You have made room to set a special place for them at your table.

Though the gospel makes it clear that VIP kids need to be a priority, not all churches embrace this opportunity. One mom shares her raw feelings. (Warning! This is not meant to be offensive, but reveals the hurt and frustration of a parent of a child with disability.)

Our church has a wonderful children's ministry, but my son has been left behind. Unfortunately, the same thing that has happened to my family seems to happen to a lot of other families with special needs children—the church is the last place that one finds understanding, compassion or a helping hand. (I have had store clerks whom we don't know be more understanding and compassionate toward us.) We have been very alone in this; thank God for my mother, or we would not be able to attend church at all. The head of our children's ministry is a loving woman, who is overworked, and there is no one else who really cares about my son (or us/our struggles) at our church. Our church is too "busy" with the needs of those who don't attend to worry about the mission field right under their noses. I wish that I could say that I had the energy to be "the one" to start this special needs ministry at our church, but I was just diagnosed with lupus after 26 years of suffering (pain and extreme fatigue); my marriage is in shambles, and I have to talk myself through each and every task throughout the day because I am so exhausted, and because there is no one else to do everything that a mom and wife need to do.

In Matthew 25:40, Jesus reminds us, "Truly I tell you, whatever you did for one of the least of these brothers and sisters of mine, you did for me."

This Scripture is not meant to offend those who have disabilities, show disrespect or portray a condescending attitude toward those with special needs. This Scripture reminds us that the Body is composed of stronger parts and weaker parts. Those of us who are stronger have the responsibility to uphold and assist the weaker parts. Families that are impacted with disability, like this mom, may represent the weaker part. Our assignment is to bring strength, encouragement, practical support and hope to this part of the Body as we cheer them on their journey. It's our job to "give them Jesus!"

But how do we "give them Jesus" if we can't get over our own fears and feelings of inadequacy? How do we offer a cup of cold water to someone we may not feel equipped to help? If we don't feel equipped, does that mean it's someone else's job?

Years ago, I was asked to do a denominational workshop on including kids with special needs in ministry. Excited to have this opportunity to share my newfound passion, I diligently pored over preparation for my presentation. When the day finally arrived, with PowerPoint in place and notes in hand, I eagerly anticipated the arrival of my attendees . . . and I waited and waited and waited. To my disappointment, no one showed up.

Why does reaching out to kids with special needs seem not so important? Why do churches think it's not their ministry assignment, but rather the responsibility of the church down the street to invite these special kids to their table? Why do we focus our attention on captivating the crowds instead of pursuing ministry to the one in real need? After all, didn't Jesus choose to leave the masses and go after the one who nobody else was paying attention to? His focus was on the individual. Maybe if we began to look at kids with special needs as individuals who need Jesus, instead of a group of kids with a syndrome that we don't understand and who make us feel uncomfortable, we wouldn't be so scared to embrace them the way the gospel directs us to.

Kids with special needs are kids. Period. Their disability is not what defines them. They are not mistakes; they are kids created in the image of God who have a place in the Body of Christ. There are things that our son, Nathaniel, could teach us and reflect about the character of God that our fully abled daughters could not. He taught me about loving unconditionally, persevering and serving with no limits.

VIP kids can add value to your ministry. As they come to the table, they bring valuable gifts to fulfill their role in the Body. God has used VIP kids to teach me some valuable lessons. They have taught me that it's okay to be who you are. I have learned not to judge others, but to love them as they are.

Kids with Down syndrome have shown me how to embrace and love "the untouchables" or those who some might deem difficult to love. They bring joy everywhere they go. As I have watched VIP kids unashamedly worship God wholeheartedly, I have been inspired to embrace God more boldly in my own life. Higher functioning kids on the autism spectrum reveal the intellectual brilliance of God. The innocence of kids with intellectual disabilities allows them to be a child forever and remind me of the importance of having childlike faith to enter the kingdom of God. Kids with ADHD have taught me patience and brought out my own creative abilities in teaching. Lower functioning kids with physical disabilities remind me of my need for God in my own life and help me to forgive more quickly.

When we do not intentionally include "those" kids into our lives and ministry, we are potentially missing valuable lessons to be learned, because a valuable part of the Body is missing.

Church is the perfect setting for typical children to learn how to interact with those touched by disability.

It's a place to ask questions and learn about compassion and service. It can be a time where kids learn that church is a place for all to worship and bring their unique gifts to the table. So how can we prepare that seat so they can fit at our table and have a place to belong?

There are many ways to make a place for kids with special needs.

When considering how to be more intentional to include VIP kids in your ministry, there are three practical models to consider:

1. Inclusion
2. Self-contained classes
3. Reverse mainstreaming

Let's briefly take a look at these three options.

Inclusion invites VIP kids to participate in every part of your children's ministry like any other child. It is best accomplished by having a Buddy volunteer accompany the child and work on adapting lessons and activities. They are able to provide one-on-one attention to the child. You will find that most parents desire that their child be included and have the same opportunities as their fellow peers.

Self-contained classes are set in place when Inclusion is not possible. Overstimulating environments or physical and/or behavioral issues might warrant a classroom or space that can be adopted for VIP kids to maximize their learning experience. Having some basic sensory activities can help children focus and actually learn better. Special Education teachers or therapists can offer suggestions of what activities might be helpful and inexpensive to create. Parents can also share ideas about what modifications can be helpful for their child.

Reverse mainstreaming is when you invite fully abled kids to rotate in and join VIP kids who are not participating in the typical kids' church setting. This allows kids to have interaction with each other but in a setting that will be more conducive for VIP kids.

As you consider these models, remember that there is no disabled soul; kids can experience and learn about the love of God at any level.

Ministering to kids with special needs is only part of the equation when considering a special needs ministry, as special needs impact the entire family. Churches not only need to consider how to minister to the special needs child who is coming, but considerations and provisions must also be made for the siblings and caregivers. If we are not careful, these needs can go unnoticed as families sit in silence, quietly overwhelmed.

How would ministry Jesus-style respond to the following real-life situations?

Elizabeth struggles to keep her two boys happy and quiet through a church service. They do not attend kids' church because no one has really let them know that they are welcome to attend. For years this single mom has quietly slipped in and out of service on Sunday morning with oxygen tank in tow. People awkwardly smile and move on to leave her to work it out on her own.

Joe and Mary have not been able to attend church together for years. Every week they take turns going to church because their son Jason has autism and they can't find a church that knows how to care for him.

Jennifer and Aaron are discouraged. They feel like a burden as they try to find a church that will look at their child as an individual and not a casualty. They struggle to find a place, as a family, to belong. As they do so, their older son's needs go unmet as he is not able to get grounded in a viable kids' ministry.

Why do parents have to fight to get their kids noticed?

Somehow this is not what I think Jesus intended or what churches really want to happen. Not knowing what to do sometimes paralyzes us from doing anything. When churches decide that its time to provide intentional ministry, lives are changed.

We have found that one practical way to provide intentional ministry is to start a respite care program. Respite is simply a parents-day-out program for VIP kids and siblings that allows kids to have fun and provides targeted ministry opportunities; and parents can get a much-needed break that is often so hard to find. It also creates community that gives these families a special place to belong. These families don't need a potluck to attend; they need rest. The gospel is practical. Offering a cup of cold water is practical. Reaching out with respite care is giving a cup of cold water to VIP families.

Matt has three VIP girls—two on the autism spectrum and one with Down syndrome. He is a sports writer whose job takes him on the road many weeks out of the year. This can be challenging and overwhelming for his wife (his girls' stepmom). This letter was sent to me in response to an inquiry I made as I routinely checked up on this family:

We have almost nowhere to turn and we are in a situation that is extremely trying. Madeline was up most of last night screaming. Molly was up the night before, yelping. Meghan is home with the flu, but is nonverbal, so we didn't know she was sick until she was very sick.

As you know, this is sooooo tiring. And I like to think I have endless energy and hope. But . . . I do not. So I need to reach out to others for help. As I see it, we are all one big family when it comes to raising Meghan, Molly and Maddie. Matt and I are the everyday people, and you are the line behind us. You all are what give us strength to get up every night with one or all of them. When we see something in the paper about parents who lose it, we always say, "Why didn't they ask for help?" and so I am saying "*help*" . . . yet so few care to hear us. But you all do, and it's appreciated more than can be expressed. I need to just have quiet sometimes—to clear my head and to not be responsible. I need to sit down and eat. I need to take a shower. I need to see my husband as a husband and not a fellow caretaker. When he is away, I need to regroup and start over and get my house cleaned and ready for the rest of the weekend. We need to go to the store and be able to shop and stay at the store for as long as we need to without leaving because of a tantrum.

It's actually vital to us as a functioning family. We moved here for school.

We have no family here that can help us. You have become our family. And we now rely upon you as family.

Through churches providing respite care, Matt and his family have found a place to belong and now receive meaningful ministry. They have found a home in the church that initially reached out to them at their point of need through a respite care program. People from the church have found a way to engage with this family in need. Volunteers have gotten over their own fears about disability and can now be more ready to engage with VIP kids in other ways, inside and outside of the church.

Ministering to families with children with disabilities is a long-term commitment. It's serving like Jesus. He did not come to be served, but to serve, and to give His life a ransom for many. It can take you out of your box and be inconvenient at times. Remember that many parents are on this journey for the first time and are learning about the uniqueness of their child as well. Their child was not born with an instruction manual. As children grow, adjustments must be made. In some cases, children may never experience independence. Caregivers need Jesus "in the flesh" to help them not grow weary on this journey.

So now that you are willing, and contemplating being more intentional about ministry to kids with special needs and their families, where do you begin? Here are some practical tips to getting started:

1. Take a deep breath and pray. Ask God to help you. He loves VIP kids more than you can imagine. His heart is to reach these kids and families, and He will help you be His hands and heart to do so.
2. Face your own fears and feelings of intimidation about disability. One of the best ways to do this is to invest in a VIP kid! Schedule a visit to a child's home or school. Get to know about his or her disability, equipment and needs. You will learn a lot by spending time with the child in his or her normal environment. As you do so, you will lead the way for others to follow your example.
3. Remember that the parents are your best coach. Talk to them about their child. Get to know them. Partner with them on their journey. Developing a child profile might be helpful to you and your volunteer team. Don't reinvent the wheel. There are some great resources out there.
4. Think outside the box. To provide intentional ministry, you may have to change the way you have always done things.
5. Just start somewhere! Don't worry about putting together a polished plan. Just start looking at the kids God has brought to you and find a way to take care of them. As you do so, you can develop your strategy to include more kids and spread the word.

If you do not have any VIP kids, do a survey to find them. They may be in your congregation and not coming because they may not know they can. Find a special needs walk or service project and get involved. There is an abundance of kids in our community.

As you intentionally invite families in, educate your congregation about the needs of VIP families. Tell their stories. Share their needs and prayer requests. Help them understand God's heart on reaching and supporting this part of the Body. You will be surprised at the most unlikely candidates that will respond.

Try to be practical. Anticipate the needs of your VIP families. As you consider how to minister to the VIP child who is coming, considerations and provisions should also be made for the sibling. Siblings often grow up quickly at a young age as they are put in a caregiver role. The demands in the home may not allow them to participate in normal kid or church activities. Is there a practical way that you can assist so that siblings can participate? It might be something as simple as providing transportation to church. Be intentional to reach out! Think through your special events and how to make it possible for VIP kids to participate. Something as simple as having Buddy volunteers available for special events can be helpful.

Love in practical ways.

As you set your table with a special place and venture out to do what the Bible instructs us to do, be assured that a special needs ministry will bring back blessings you may never have anticipated! "He who waters others will himself be watered" (Prov. 11:2).

All of God's kids are created with value and purpose, regardless of their abilities or capabilities. Man looks on the outside, but God looks on the heart. He sees possibilities in all of us.

Our son, Nathaniel, had a change of address at age four and a half, and now he lives in heaven. God has woven purpose into his life, and today his life continues to impact thousands. I am so glad that Jesus made a special seat for Nathaniel at His table. Who is the gospel for? It's for kids . . . "those" kids. Let's "give them Jesus"!

DISCUSSION QUESTIONS

1. What is your greatest fear of working with kids with special needs?
2. What is one practical thing you can do to help bridge the gap to kids with disabilities in your own life?
3. Describe a time when you didn't know how to respond to a child with special needs.
4. What are some ways that you can move your ministry from being tolerant to intentional?
5. What do you think of the statement that not all churches are called to special needs ministry?

8

Partnering with the Youth Ministry

CHAD MILLER

Ordained in 2000 as a nondenominational preacher of the gospel, Chad serves as director of Children's and Youth Evangelism Training with the Billy Graham Evangelistic Association (BGEA), and as an associate pastor at West Cabarrus Church in Concord, North Carolina.

In addition to directing the creation and publishing of *Dare to Be a Daniel* five-session curriculum (ages 10–14) and BGEA's *The Greatest Journey* (ages 6–10), Chad also serves as an instructor for BGEA's Christian Life & Witness Course and BGEA's FM419 Youth Training.

Chad has served with BGEA for 10 years. He loves to see believers equipped for the work of ministry—making disciples for life!

Chad's 18-plus years of family/congregational ministry have helped shape his biblical perspective on the leadership needs within the local church. He is currently working toward his master's degree in Christian ministry from Charlotte Bible College and Seminary with a double emphasis in biblical theology and ministry.

Chad and his wife of 15 years, Ashlie, live near Kannapolis, North Carolina, with their three young sons.

Recent Articles Published

- Children's Pastors' *Insight* E-magazine
- ChurchLeaders.com
- *KidzMatter Magazine*

Recent Keynote/Seminars

- Children's Pastors' Conference, Orlando, Florida and San Diego, California
- Christian Camp and Conference Association National Convention
- Northwest Ministry Conference, Seattle, Washington

Sessions Taught

- From Sunday School to Real Life
- Making Modern-Day Missionaries
- Reaching Tweens with the Gospel
- Getting the Gospel Beyond the Campfire (equipping campers for gospel work)
- Understanding and Ministering to the Emerging Generation
- Reclaiming Youth Ministry for Making Disciples
- The Art of Presentation
- Prayer that Mobilizes Ministry

For the last several years of serving both in a parachurch organization, whose work is mostly proclamation evangelism and evangelism training, and as an associate pastor in some variation at a local church, I've had two distinct vantage points to observe the trends and activities in the children's ministry movement. The two distinctions *could* be summarized as the theoretical/theological and the practical/biographical expression of those ideas. I must say, we have seen great strides in the language of children's ministry. The youth ministry culture, and its growing diversity, appears to be a microcosm of the church's seismic variations both within and across denominational lines.

A major concern that must be addressed and will have generational consequences is that, at least in the mainstream ministry culture, there is such a wall of separation between the two ministries—that is, between the children's area and the youth area. It's as though they operate with separate agendas, separate philosophies, separate communication flows, separate ministry objectives, separate metrics of success. Thus, they are reaping quite different harvests.

Reaping What We've Sown in the Last 15 to 20 Years

We've all read the same stats, surveys and studies—they're not revealing much in the way of earthshaking revelation.

- We know that an overwhelming majority of our children coming up through church are walking away from the church and what they know of Christianity as quickly as they can around the age of 18.
- We know that while a large majority of Americans identify themselves as "Christian," roughly 4 percent or so actually possess a biblical worldview that affects the way they live their lives.

The term "nominal Christian" has recently gained prominence in referring to those individuals who identify themselves as Christians but have little internal convictions, a high degree of biblical illiteracy and are virtually indistinguishable in lifestyle from non-Christians. (I wonder if heaven has as many slices of Christianity as we do? Or do you suppose Jesus looks to see if anyone has repented, put their faith and trust in Him, taken up their cross and daily follows after Him?)

Nevertheless, in the midst of emerging trends in this postmodern, post-Christian culture, the call and measure of ministry (our marching orders) haven't changed. We are called to "Go therefore and make disciples of all nations" (Matt. 28:19, *ESV*). What does a fully devoted disciple of Jesus look like? I think that, at any age, it's one who loves Jesus, is actively following Him and is sharing Him with others. It's so much more than that, but at its basic definition, it is that!

I've written several times before on the strategic advantage of shifting our thinking from solely an evangelistic event as the primary means of proclamation and harvest to the training and equipping of believers to "do the work of an evangelist" (2 Tim. 4:5, *ESV*). I won't belabor the point, but peer-to-peer influence is so significant in the tween and early teen years that it's worth the blood, sweat and tears to pour into our young people to live out:

> But in your hearts revere Christ as Lord. Always be prepared to give an answer to everyone who asks you to give the reason for the hope that you have. But do this with gentleness and respect (1 Pet. 3:15).

We are now reaping the harvest of the deistic humanism (the god of self) movement of the 1960s and '70s. The frontline advocates for "my rights, my body, my choices . . . no one can tell me different . . . if it feels good, do it" are now largely in positions of influence in the halls of academia and politics, and they are the authors of many a textbook that school children are required to ingest with regularity. This movement has paved the way for the modern-day pluralism monopolizing the mainstream religious discourse.

Please understand that pluralism is not simply the recognition and acknowledgment of different faith systems within a community; it is the leveling and neutralizing of all religions for the sake of "equitable public discourse." It is the real conviction that all religions possess equal merit and benefit and are, therefore, not superior or inferior to one another—they all do the same thing with the same results. I don't think you need convincing that this is where we are in North America right now.

This Harvest's Effects on Youth Ministry

Recently, at an executive leadership gathering of various national youth ministries, the question was posed, "What's your big dream for the ministry beyond your own ministry?" As we began to share some of our answers around the table, it was quickly apparent that most of the discussion was centered on the propagation of youth ministry. Did you catch that? . . . advancing "youth ministry" as an entity, a force, a distinguished movement. My concern with this thinking is that it may not be completely in line with either Deuteronomy chapters 6 and 11, or the Titus 2 charge to have a family-centered, simultaneously multigenerational faith experience for the child. (It's worth noting that when I mention "youth ministry," I am thinking of a movement, not of students but of the publishers, parachurch organizations, evangelists, writers, ministers and other voices that might shape the latest trends and thus products/resources available and promoted to the local church.)

I continue to hear noised abroad, as do some of you, that youth ministry needs to reinvent itself. Ponderings of "What will be the next 'thing'?" "Is there untapped creativity that might take youth ministry in a brand new direction?" That was certainly a concern of some of the nation's key voices for youth ministry that were at this gathering.[1] So the grand vision I inserted (which wasn't really grand at all) was for the local church to stop viewing children and youth ministries as separate entities that are about different things. It was greeted with little to no fanfare, and we moved back to discussing the hip new reinvention of the paradigm.

But I believe youth pastors need to be communicating with children's leaders on a regular basis. Not in a "here's what I want from you" tone, but a "we both know what God requires; how will we go about making disciple-making disciples?" Children's and youth ministries need to stop cooperating with one another and start collaborating. I don't mean with respect only to the next year's curricula that will be used. I *do mean* with regard to the reality that some of the children in our classrooms, at this very moment (statistically speaking and prophetically hoping), will one day be in our positions—leading other children to Christ. *What kind of children's and youth ministry are you shaping for a generation yet to be created?*

Children's ministry (in the same way that I referred to youth ministry earlier) needs to take to heart the current dilemmas and challenges of where youth ministry is right now. Christianity doesn't need another empire built from within, which must be maintained and must constantly seek to reinvent itself as an entity. It should be an organic movement and a natural outflow of building up the Body.

Different Seasons Call for
Special Attention to Seed Sowing

So, let's assume we're all on board. We are all on the same page with the Holy Spirit in children's and youth ministry within the local church, and as loosely defined movements that exist to resource the worker. Let's imagine for a moment that these walls have been scaled. Let's envision for a moment that we have children's and youth workers collaboratively discipling young people and believing that they are capable of *doing* the work of the Kingdom while they are *learning* about the King. If we begin to systematically train and equip our students to appropriately share the glorious gospel of Jesus Christ with their friends and families, how now shall we pray for them? Is it for boldness . . . for courage . . . no fear of rejection or alienation? It's likely all of these, but it's a bit more!

We are sending out these missionaries to a land bereft of any concrete spiritual consensus! We're deploying them into a culture where "exclusivity" in religious claims is a foreign tongue. The mantra is "I'm okay; you're okay; we're all okay," as opposed to "For all have sinned and come short of the glory of God" (Rom. 3:23, *KJV*). The moment our kids confront the world with the claims of Christ, they are speaking a language that most won't hear. The language of our day is the aforementioned pluralism and relativism. Pluralism could be defined as the belief that every religion is true, that each provides a genuine encounter with the Ultimate. One may be better than the others, but all are adequate.[2] Relativism is similar to pluralism, claiming that each religion is true to the individual who holds it. Relativists believe that since there is no objective truth in religion, there are no criteria by which one can tell which religion is, or which religions are, false.[3]

The authoritative voices in our children's lives will say, "It's okay for you to believe in Jesus, but remember that he's on a level playing ground. Imagine Jesus sitting at the table with all the other religious leaders . . . and they're all talking about the right things." There is only one thing wrong with that—*everything*! Jesus Christ will never sit at the table beside Muhammad, Buddha or Confucius as a contemporary or equal—*He sits on the throne* and *there is none like him*! (See Rev. 20–21; Ps. 86:8.)

We are sending out the children and youth we minister to into an increasingly hostile environment. This is for real! Are you preparing them as disciple-making disciples with no fear of man, but a holy fear of God—or as fun-seeking adrenaline junkies who become the nice people that will check the "Christian" box of religious affiliation someday only because they haven't tried the other choices?

One of my dear friends in ministry who is now (at this writing) serving churches all over Australia as a ministry coordinator recently shared a poignant account of a turning point in his ministry. He was walking in town one day with his little girl when a young man from across the street yelled out, "Hey, Pastor Jim!" Jim[4] turned around slowly because he hadn't been called that in some time—he'd been mostly serving through parachurch organizations (not as vocational staff at a church). As he turned, the young man yelled again, "Pastor Jim! Pastor Jim!" The two were now within speaking distance.

Jim's little girl listened as the young man said he was in Jim's youth group many years before. "We had such fun . . . do you remember the crazy stuff we used to do?" Jim began to make the connection in his mind as to who this was. "Didn't we have such fun, Jim? Remember when we went to McDonalds to see who could eat the most Big Macs in one night? That was awesome!" Jim laughed. The man continued to reminisce about other games and activities that he remembered; then Jim interrupted and asked, "Hey man, whatever happened to that girl you were sweet on in youth group?"

The man's countenance dropped a bit. "Well, Jim, she fell pregnant. We had a kid together." His eyes dropped to the ground now. "We got married because that's what we thought we were supposed to do. But it didn't last; we split up pretty quick."

"I'm sorry to hear that," Jim responded.

"That's okay," the young man replied. "I got another girl pregnant and that didn't work out for us well either. Anyway . . ." he said hurriedly, "I was wondering if you could tell me where any churches are around here that were like yours."

Jim's spark of optimism at this request was quickly doused when the young man continued, "I don't really go or have any use for it, but I really want my kids to have fun like I did when I was with you. What fun we had together, Jim! It's so awesome to see you!"

As they said their goodbyes and began to go their separate ways, Jim's daughter looked at her dad and said, "Daddy, why are you crying?" Jim whimpered, "We'll talk about it later, Sweetie."

Jim shares this story with children's and youth workers all over the world to drive home his broken heart when he realized he had missed an opportunity to make disciples. He was driven by his love for young people, but he wasn't shepherding their hearts toward the King!

When the kids in your children's ministry or youth gatherings pass you on the street 10 to 15 years from now, what will they recall most from your time with them? We recognize that the Holy Spirit alone changes the hearts of men and women, and boys and girls, but what kind of table are you preparing for them to feast on: the sugar rush and flash of junk food, or the balanced meal from God's Word?

Children's ministry will do well to take note of the enterprise of youth ministry. Let us learn from and leverage the successes and drink from many wells we won't have to dig. But let us with heavenly wisdom avoid the temptation to try to create simply a better and more wholesome entertainment option for kids. Jesus is worth more than that! Let's engage and equip children and youth, and expect them to reach their friends and family with the gospel. Let's pray heaven's best for them. "And when they had prayed, the place in which they were gathered together was shaken, and they were all filled with the Holy Spirit and continued to speak the word of God with boldness" (Acts 4:31, *ESV*).

DISCUSSION QUESTIONS

1. How does our church view children's ministry? How do we measure success in our children's ministry? (Most churches are satisfied as long as the kids are happy.)
2. If we had all the money we needed, all the volunteers we needed and all the leadership support we needed, would our current model produce disciple-making disciples for Jesus?
3. Deuteronomy chapters 6 and 11 and Titus 2 communicate how to reach younger generations. What might this look like today in its simplest form? What would we need to do to equip parents to achieve these models?
4. How can we avoid the pitfalls of empire building and stay focused on advancing the kingdom of God to the ends of the earth?
5. There is no ideal setup outside of heaven. That being said, what's your big dream for your area of ministry? How is it consistent with God's Word and mission for His people?
6. The late evangelist Leonard Ravenhill said, "The world isn't wanting a new definition of Christianity, just a real demonstration of it!" How are you, as individuals, demonstrating that you belong to Jesus *outside of your roles in children's ministry?*

Notes
1. By the way, it was a wonderful gathering, and I was humbled and honored to attend. I was extremely grateful for the hospitality and for the experience and knowledge I gained being with some amazing champions for winning young people to Jesus. The chief concern and the heartbeat of everyone that I spoke with was reaching young people with the gospel and helping stimulate and be a part of expanding the kingdom of God.
2. Norman L. Geisler, *Exclusivism: The Oppositional Precondition, Systematic Theology*, (Minneapolis, MN: Bethany House, 2011), p. 93.
3. Ibid.
4. The names have been changed, but this is an actual account.

9

The Gospel in a Digital Age

MATT MCKEE

Matt is a speaker, writer, strategist and entrepreneur. A pastor in family ministry for 10 years, Matt is now combining his love of ministry with his love of business and technology. While at Fellowship Church in Grapevine, Texas, Matt helped to create and produce G-Force, a curriculum for elementary-age children. He also contributed to the dream phase of Elevate, an elementary-age curriculum currently in production. From 2005 to 2010, Matt served as pastor of students and children at Horizon Community Church in Cincinnati, Ohio. In 2010, Matt founded a mobile and social technologies company called ROAR, which produces apps and does social media consulting for nonprofit organizations. Currently, Matt leads ROAR as its CEO, as well as works with Orange, overseeing their social media strategy and mobile app initiatives.

Matt is an idea guy, preferring to let his creativity run free and see where it leads. Because of this, he might be called a serial entrepreneur. Before finding success with ROAR, he started other companies, such as Power Naming (a creative naming agency) and Chocolate Nachos (a Web design firm). Although he stays busy with ROAR and Orange, he also has a million other ideas that he's just waiting for an opportunity to make happen!

Matt wrote *Be Social: The Social Media Handbook for Churches,* which can be downloaded for free on his blog (listed below). Additionally, he consults with businesses, nonprofits, and individuals to create and maintain social media strategies that utilize social networking platforms. Matt says, "Strategy is more important than just doing. If you're trying to leverage social media for business or personal use, my best advice is to be human."

Matt believes strongly in the power of human relationships, so he seeks to build a network everywhere he goes. He is very blessed to be able to name three men as his personal mentors: Jon Heidtke, who is the general manger of Fox Sports; John Weber, who was the chaplain of the Dallas Cowboys before his death in 2007; and Richard Palmer, who is president of Nehemiah Manufacturing. Because so many great people have poured into his life, he also seeks to give back as much as he can in many different ways.

Matt resides in Cumming, Georgia, with his wife, Jessica, and two sons, Patriot and Azlan.

Blog: http://www.mattmckee.me
Facebook: http://www.facebook.com/mckeelive
Twitter: @mattmckee
YouTube: http://www.youtube.com/user/remixkids
SMS: Google Voice number: (678) 701-7047
Google+: http://gplus.to/mattmckee
Instagram: http://instagram.com/mattmckee

Once upon a time, in 1983, there was a little boy. He was a dreamer who came up with the wildest ideas! He was so curious that he drove his mother crazy with questions, and he dreamed that one day he would have the ability to find the answer to any question at the tip of his fingers. He watched *Star Wars*, and that was his only idea of what space might be like; he looked up to the sky and wished he knew more about what was really out there! He dreamed of having a magical communication device he could hold in his pocket that would allow him to talk to his friends from anywhere. He dreamed of having a camera that could capture an image the way it actually looked in real life and not just a grainy, faded replication. He dreamed of being able to watch *Star Wars* at home, or even in the car, the way it looked in the movie theater. He dreamed of a radio station that he could make play only the songs he liked, so he did not have to listen to his sister's sappy music! He dreamed of being able to touch a wall and change its color. He dreamed the craziest things, and his parents just shook their heads.

But now, a mere 30 years later, every one of that boy's dreams has become a reality. The Internet gives us access to every possible piece of information at our fingertips. Space has been much more fully explored and understood, and we can access all of those images on the Internet as well. Cell phones allow us to talk to anyone, anywhere. Cameras are crisp and high-definition, and you can view your photographs instantly without having to wait for them to be developed. High-definition movies can be streamed onto any connected device to be played anywhere. iPods and streaming music services allow us to completely customize our music playlists. Touchscreens allow us to customize even the walls around us!

With the extreme advances in technology in just a few decades, it feels like there is no dream that cannot be achieved! There are some dreams that have not been realized, but we know it is just a matter of time.

The children of today will never know what it feels like to be that little boy. Technology makes every dream possible.

Today's Digital World

We live in a connected world: computers, cell phones, tablets, smartphones . . . And now with wearable tech, like smart watches, smart glasses and smart shoes, technology is becoming more and more a part of who we are and what we do—not to mention social media sites like Facebook, Twitter, Pinterest, Tumblr, Instagram and blogs. Like it or not, the world in which today's children are growing up is a digitally connected one, beyond what many of us could have ever imagined when we were kids.

Some Simple Facts About Today's World

1. In 2012, there were 2.5 billion Internet users in the world, a full third of the global population.[1] In the United States, 90 percent of the population is on the Internet.[2]
2. The number of mobile devices in use in the world, including feature phones, smartphones, and tablets, is more than 7 billion, exceeding the entire population of the world.[3]
3. At the end of 2012, there were 1.5 billion smartphones in use worldwide. The number is expected to hit 2 billion before 2015.[4]
4. In March of 2013:

   - Facebook was by far the biggest social site, with 1.06 billion active monthly users, 680 million mobile users, more than 50 million pages and 10 million apps.[5] This means that if Facebook were a nation, it would have the third largest population in the world, only smaller than China and India.[6]
   - Twitter had more than 200 million active users.
   - YouTube had 1 billion users with 4 billion daily views.
   - Pinterest had 48.7 million users.
   - Instagram had 100 million users with 4 billion uploaded photos.

5. In today's world, it is easier to get a cell phone than to get clean water.

The purpose of all these statistics is simply to drive home the point that our world is a technological one, and technology is what today's children know. Nowadays, people leave the house with three things: money, keys and phone (and money is slowly becoming replaced by a digital wallet!). The mobile phone has become a necessary part of a person's daily ensemble, and many people panic if their phone is unavailable for any reason.

So the fact that technology is an integral part of today's world is established. But what does that mean for ministry? Well, the fact is that Jesus is Lord over every aspect of our lives. Just as He asks us to give Him our time, talents and resources, He asks us to give Him our technology too. He can and will use technology to impact ministry just like He will use anything else.

Technology and Real Relationships

"What you see is what you get." This is a common phrase in our culture, and it underscores the fact that people often trust what their eyes see as being true or genuine, rather than the things people say. However, when you are using technology to communicate, your eyes cannot see the other person, so how do you know for sure what you are getting? This is one argument that many people have against embracing the use of technology and online tools in building relationships—it feels fake since you are not interacting with a person face to face.

However, this is just not the case with today's young people. For them, the use of texting and Facebook are completely natural, and that is how you communicate. For people who love and want to reach young people, this is just something they are going to have to get used to. People in the early 1900s probably thought that the telephone was an extremely awkward and unnatural way to communicate with loved ones. However, it caught on, people got used to it and it became entirely mainstream in modern culture.

In 2012, 78 percent of teens aged 12 to 17 had a cell phone, half of whom had smartphones.[7] At that time, teens sent and received an average of 60 texts a day, with the heaviest users sending well over 200 texts a day. It has also been noted that with the increase of texting among young people, the prevalence of voice calls has diminished.[8] Texting has become the preferred method of communication among teenagers in the United States. This just shows that young people do not have the same distrust of technology that adults tend to have when it comes to communicating with their friends. It also follows logically that younger children will be even more comfortable with the use of technology when they gain access to things like cell phones and social media, so older people who love them will need to learn to use the communication methods that they are most comfortable with.

The truth is that technology is not meant to replace offline relationships, but just enhance them. For teenagers, texting does not replace talking to a friend whenever they are together. It is just a way for them to continue communicating even when they cannot be together. Facebook does not keep teens from telling their friends about an event, but it does make sure the friends know about it even if they cannot hear about it in person right then. Technological means do not replace face-to-face communication, but they allow people to stay connected even when they are not physically together. Because of this, one may argue that technology allows friends to be even closer because they know more about what is happening to each other even when they cannot be there to witness it in person.

Although technological communication may feel unnatural to those who did not grow up using it, the trend is mostly that people are honest and genuine in the way they present themselves on social media. In fact, most people go much further in sharing their true selves in the "safe" zone behind a screen rather than the scary zone of looking someone in the eyes. "Oversharing" has become a common word in today's world because many young people tend to share too much personal information in the public format of social media. So, although you cannot see a person's face to know exactly what he or she meant when the message was sent, you can trust that it was probably sent with no intention to deceive.

The kind of openness and connectedness fostered by digital communication is really valuable to relationships and can be used for great good by people who have good intentions. It is a fast and simple way to get a great message out to a large number of people, and it is also a good way to get a feel for how a person is doing and what he or she is dealing with at this time in his or her life.

Confronting the Dark Side

You may have noticed the sentence in the previous paragraph that says "[Digital communication] can be used for great good by people who have good intentions." Another argument that many people have against embracing technological communication is that some people use it with very bad intentions, for very harmful purposes. Pastors blame Facebook for divorces. Parents are shocked to find their teenagers using cell phones to send sexual text messages ("sexting"). Violent people use Twitter to stir up riots that damage property and harm people. Predators use online chat forums to find unsuspecting victims. The list could go on and on of the heartbreaking things that people use technology to accomplish. The essential thing to remember, though, is that it is people who are doing these terrible things, not the technology.

An important principle when it comes to technology and social media is that they are just communication tools—nothing more, nothing less. Technology itself is amoral, neither good nor bad. It is the people using the tools who make it either good or bad. Consider the example of another kind of tool: a knife. In the hands of a surgeon, a knife can do great good. In the hands of a killer, a knife can do great evil. In both of those cases, though, it is not the knife that takes the credit or the blame; it is the person wielding it. In the hands of most people, a knife does nothing greater than slice bread or open a package. In the same way, depending on who uses it, technology can do either great good or great evil, but most uses of technology are just inconsequential.

Technology and social media cannot be blamed for the harm that evil people use them to cause. When in the hands of people with good intentions, technology can also be used for great good. So, rather than boycotting these powerful communication tools and abandoning them to only evil purposes, a bolder choice would be to claim them for good instead. Make a decision to do as much good with them as you can, choosing to spread light rather than allowing darkness to reign.

Remember, technology does not make its own choices for good or for bad. It is people who make the choices of how to use it, and people who do not know the Savior will typically not make the choice to always use it for good. Let us use people's preferred methods of communication to help spread the love and truth of the gospel rather than allowing sin and darkness to claim total power in these popular arenas.

Using technology does not make you a "techie." It just makes you a person who reaches out to people in whatever way they can best understand. You are not in the tech business; you are in the people business.

What Does This Have to Do with Children's Ministry?

As convincing as the argument may be about today's technological world, most children do not carry around cell phones, and most of the social networks restrict registration to people over age 13. So do those in children's ministry need to be concerned about using technology to reach out? The answer is yes, and there are two very good reasons.

First, as mentioned previously, today's teenagers prefer texting and Facebook over any other method of communication, and so it follows that younger children will be even more comfortable communicating on technology as they get older. They may not be on Facebook now, but they know all about Facebook, and they will sign up as soon as their parents allow them to (which is often much younger than 13).[9] They may not carry a cell phone now, but they text with their parents' phones or have their parents send messages for them. These kids have never known a world without smartphones and social media. They are more comfortable on an iPad than most of the adults they know. They love video games, smartphones and tablets, and they will spend as much time on them as their parents will allow. You do not have to like the fact that today's children are digital communicators, but if you want to be seen as relevant and be effective at reaching them, you are going to have to accept it.

The second reason that technology is a vital part of children's ministry is that these kids have parents/guardians. Most of the time, the adult caregivers in a child's life are the gateway to reaching children or even allowing them to participate in church events at all. If you are going to reach the kids, you have to reach the parents. Parents of young children are probably young enough themselves that they have already embraced technology and social media, so that is a great place to start trying to reach them.

Parents of older children, however, may be bewildered at their tech-savvy children. What better place than the church for these parents to learn how to reach their own children? They need to be assured that the technological divide is not uncrossable! If parents see a minister embracing digital communication, they may be more willing to try it themselves. A minister can also help educate parents about how to use technology, how to instruct their children in its safe use, and how to use it to positively impact their children.

There is such great potential for technology as a place where great good can be done! It is time for those in ministry to seize it and run with it.

Where to Start

For those who have not embraced technology and social media from the start, it can be overwhelming to even know where to start. You do not have to have the latest gadget or most expensive piece of technology. You just need a computer or device with Internet access, some kind of cell phone and a willing heart. You are most likely already using email and a cell phone for ministry, so it is not much of a jump to embrace technology the way people are using it.

It may help to view yourself as a digital missionary. In that sense, you want to learn the digital culture of the community you would like to reach. Is your target community composed of parents, siblings or even older kids themselves? Do some research to find out what social networks they use and how they use them. One extremely simple way to do this is to take a survey. Ask people to answer a few questions about their use of social media and what they would be interested in using in regard to your ministry. Ask questions like:

- What social networks do you use regularly?
- What do you use social networks for?
- How much time per day do you spend on social networks?
- If this ministry had a Facebook page/Twitter account, would you follow it?
- What kind of content would you enjoy seeing on Facebook/Twitter from this ministry?
- Would you be interested in receiving text messages from this ministry?

Once you have a feel for the digital culture of your community, you join in where most of your community is. Just like a missionary, you join the community, become a part of a culture and then show Jesus to that culture.

It is not as frightening to get started on a social media network as it may seem. Each particular network asks a specific question when you are posting on it, so that can be your guide in figuring out how to use each site.

Facebook asks, "What's on your mind?" so that means you use it to post your thoughts and feelings. Facebook is mostly about who you are.

Twitter asks, "What's happening?" so that means you use it to post daily events. The 140-character limit means you cannot post deep thoughts, but you can post frequent, short updates about what is going on at the time.

Pinterest asks, "What are you looking at?" so you use it to share interesting things you see online.

Instagram asks, "What photos are you taking?" so you use it to share photos of whatever you are doing at the time.

YouTube asks, "What videos are you taking?" so you use it to share videos of whatever you are doing at the time.

Google+ asks, "What's new?" so you use it to share both thoughts/feelings and current events.

Tumblr asks, "What are you creating?" so you use it to share photos, links, music, quotes, videos, anything that you have put together to express any kind of thought.

LinkedIn asks, "Who are you connected with?" so you use it to allow people to know who you are associated with.

FourSquare asks, "Where are you?" so you use it to check into current locations.

The Gospel Is Worth It

For a person who is not into technology and social media, this may seem like a whole lot of hassle. However, the plain truth is that the gospel is worth it. Today's world is online, and it is connected. Simply put, if you want to exponentially expand your ministry's reach to families and children, technological resources will allow you to do it.

Consider the example of Northland Church (http://www.northland church. net), based in Florida. Its full name is "Northland, A Church Distributed" because it considers itself a worldwide church. There are three main meeting locations in Florida, but it streams online five full worship services every week that thousands of individuals and home groups participate in from all over the world. In addition to the streamed services, they have a vibrant Facebook community (http://www.facebook.com/northlandchurch) that reaches thousands. This church is a great example of how digital tools can be used to greatly multiply a church's reach and ministry.

Consider another nonprofit organization called Global Media Outreach (GMO) (http://globalmediaoutreach.com/), which operates entirely online. GMO recognizes that many people across the globe use the convenience and accessibility of the Internet to search for answers to spiritual questions, and so they work hard to make sure that those people find answers. They maintain many websites that present the truth of the gospel in various formats, and then they use search engines and advertising on other sites to help people find those sites. In 2011 alone, GMO presented the gospel to more than 145 million people through more than 100 different websites globally. Of those, more than 19 million people indicated a decision for Christ. GMO also has trained volunteers who then follow up with new believers for discipleship over email.

These stories are inspiring, but do not be overwhelmed. Your ministry on technology and social media does not have to be this huge to make a difference. In your very community, teenagers are searching for identity and affirmation; parents are desperate to reach their kids but do not know how; children just want to have fun but are naive to the dangers that could await them. All of these are places where a loving ministry could make a huge difference in one life or in many. Just step out, take a risk and put the truth of God's love out there. In today's world, you never know who you might reach.

The Digital Gospel

It is time to erase the post-Christian message in the modern era that says faith is outdated, that people no longer need God. There does not have to be a divide between faith and modern culture. It is up to the church to show people how faith can still be relevant. The church can push the boundaries of both technology and the gospel to really settle in a place where people are. The church *can* be relevant and reach people exactly where they are. It will take time and effort, but it will pay off immensely.

The gospel may look different in a digital format than it used to before technology. Being effective on social media does not mean posting 20 Bible verses every day and hoping people read and understand them. Instead, it requires being a real person, caring about others and modeling what a genuine Christian life looks like. Interaction is one key to success in digital formats, partly for the reason expressed in the beginning of this chapter—you cannot see each other face to face, so you have to go further to make sure your communication was received correctly.

Living a digital gospel means:

- *Being real.* Share honest thoughts even if they are hard. If you are struggling with something, share about it. People will be more comfortable in their own skin if they realize that everyone else struggles the same way they do.
- *Being caring.* If a person shares a status about something difficult, post a comment that you are praying for them, then actually pray for them, and then follow up later asking how it is going.
- *Being available.* It will not help if you make social media accounts but never use them. It will take time to maintain them, and you need to

check in often. If you do not, you may miss entirely a situation that you could have made a difference in.

- *Having fun.* Being boring does not make the gospel look very appealing. Not all of your social media posts have to be about the Bible or church. If they are, the people who could most benefit from your ministry will probably not follow you at all. Share about things like a fun activity your family did together, a great meal you ate, or a prank some of the kids pulled on you.

One interesting trend that happened during the season of Lent in 2013 is that many people chose to fast from social media rather than a physical treat like chocolate or soft drinks.[10] This is very telling because it shows that people value and enjoy social media as much as chocolate, which is a lot. It also shows that people recognize how powerful social media is, and that sometimes it is good to step back and make sure the amount of power it has in your own life is healthy.

It is a fine balance to walk, but the Church should be right in the middle of the places where people are trying to figure out the best way to live. Rather than leaving people to figure out technology for themselves, the digital gospel means the Church rolls up its sleeves and helps them figure it out.

The Great Commission that Christ gave His followers before He left earth was this:

> Go and make disciples of all nations, baptizing them in the name of the Father and of the Son and of the Holy Spirit, and teaching them to obey everything I have commanded you (Matt. 28:19-20).

In our digital world, disciples can be made through technology, and obedience to Christ can be lived out digitally. It is up to the Church to be present in those digital places and help people figure out what it means to be a follower of Christ in the digital age. It may be an unknown, scary place, but Christ calls us to be bold in our ministry. The key to our courage can be found in the rest of verse 20:

> And surely I am with you always, to the very end of the age (Matt. 28:20).

We do not have to be afraid, because Christ promises to be with us always. Ask Him for help as you navigate the murky waters of the digital age. He completely understands everything about technology and social media, and if you commit to Him what you do, He will establish your plans (see Prov. 16:3).

DISCUSSION QUESTIONS

1. What keeps our ministry from innovation?
2. What problems do we have that are already solved by technology but we are either afraid to use it or simply do not know how?
3. Where can we find the resources (a knowledgeable person, a book to read, a website to access, and so on) to help us overcome that barrier?
4. What if we could reach more people online than we could offline? Would we focus more of our time there?
5. Can our ministry benefit from spending more time on digital ministry? Who on our team (staff and/or volunteers) would be good at digital ministry?
6. Why does the Internet get such a bad name? How does our community feel about the Internet, technology and social media?
7. Are there any technology-related problems in our community that we could help conquer by becoming involved?
8. If we were to begin using social media to minister, what network would we start with? Who would be our target community? What would we use social media to communicate to them?
9. How can we look at social media being more about people than media?

Notes
1. "Internet Users in the World: Distribution by World Regions," *Internet World Stats*, 2012. http://www.internetworldstats.com/stats.htm (accessed October 2013).
2. "Internet Users in North America," *Internet World Stats*, June 30, 2012. http://www.internetworldstats.com/stats14.htm (accessed October 2013).
3. Charles Arthur, "Mobile Internet Devices 'Will Outnumber Humans this Year'," *The Guardian*, February 7, 2013. http://www.guardian.co.uk/technology/2013/feb/07/mobile-internet-outnumber-people (accessed October 2013).
4. Heather Leonard, "There Will Soon Be One Smartphone for Every Five People in the World," *Business Insider*, February 7, 2013. http://www.businessinsider.com/15-billion-smartphones-in-the-world-22013-2 (accessed October 2013).

5. Craig Smith, "How Many People Use the Top Social Media, Apps & Services?" *Digital Marketing Ramblings*, September 15, 2013. http://expandedramblings.com/index.php/resource-how-many-people-use-the-top-social-media/ (accessed October 2013).

6. "The World Populations and the Top Ten Countries with the Highest Population," *Internet World Stats*, June 30, 2012. http://www.internetworldstats.com/stats8.htm (accessed October 2013).

7. Mary Madden, Amanda Lenhart, Maeve Duggan, Sandra Cortesi and Urs Gasser, "Teens and Technology 2013," *Pew Internet*, March 13, 2013. http://www.pewinternet.org/Reports/2013/Teens-and-Tech/Summary-of-Findings.aspx (accessed October 2013).

8. Amanda Lenhart, "Teens, Smartphones & Texting," *Pew Internet*, March 19, 2013. http://www.pewinternet.org/~/media/Files/Reports/2012/PIP_Teens_Smartphones_and_Texting.pdf (accessed October 2013).

9. Zoe Fox, "38% of Children on Facebook Are Younger Than 12," *Mashable*, April 11, 2012. http://mashable.com/2012/04/11/children-on-facebook/ (accessed October 2013).

10. Camille Bautista, "Is Social Media the New Chocolate During Lent?" *Mashable*, March 26, 2013. http://mashable.com/2013/03/26/social-media-lent/ (accessed October 2013.)

PART 3:

Who Shares the Gospel with Children?

10

How to Effectively Share the Gospel with Children

JOHN AND CRYSTAL MCLENNAN

John and Crystal McLennan are pastors at a church in Houston, Texas. They have a passion for ministering to children and families, and they enjoy traveling to speak at kids camps, family services and children's ministry events. They have both served in youth and children's ministry for more than 10 years. They have a Yorkie named Charlie, and love running, going to coffee shops and reading books. They first met in the church nursery. They both learned about Jesus and what He did for them, and at a young age they accepted Him as their savior. But at the age of five, they were separated when John's family moved away. Time passed, but through the years their lives followed a similar path. As elementary-age kids, they both served on their respective church puppet teams and learned about ministering to children. As adults, both decided to go to Bible college and dedicated their lives to full-time ministry. Crystal went to Rhema Bible College in Oklahoma, and John went to Central Bible College in Missouri. After graduation, both became pastors to youth and children. After 20 years, their seemingly separate lives merged when their parents reconnected through a mutual friend. They fell in love and got married. John and Crystal McLennan currently serve together as children's pastors. Please visit their website at www.ministrymotivator.com.

One of the most exciting times of ministering to children is watching them respond to the gospel and give their lives to Jesus. Of all the ministries in the church that focus on repairing broken lives, we get the privilege of sharing the gospel with an important group of people who have their entire lives to live for Jesus!

Presenting the gospel to children can sometimes feel overwhelming, but the Holy Spirit helps us when we rely on Him. It is interesting that the way God set it up is for people to reach people. It is the Holy Spirit who does the work (see 2 Thess. 2:13-14), but it is our responsibility to open our mouths and preach the gospel (see Rom. 10:14). But have no fear! This chapter will give you some practical ideas and creative methods to effectively share the gospel with children. This could happen in the context of a church service, an outreach event in the community, or in talking with a child or family individually.

The Truth of the Gospel

Children have great faith and can also understand much more than we sometimes give them credit for. When presenting the gospel to children, it is vital that we relate to them the truths of the gospel in a way they understand and can apply to their lives. At the same time, we need to be careful in the search for simplicity to not water down or omit important essentials. Here are some essentials to include so that we build a solid foundation (see Matt. 7:25), no matter what method is used:

1. *The Bible is God's Word.* It is completely true, and it gives us the truth about who Jesus is, how we are created special by God, and how we can live our lives for Him (see 2 Tim. 3:16). It is not just a storybook or fairy tale, but the ultimate truth.
2. *Everyone has sinned and come short of what God requires* (see Rom. 3:23). Sin is simply disobeying God. Have you ever lied? Stolen something? Disobeyed your mom or dad? Wanted something that didn't belong to you? Murdered someone? Wait a minute! Maybe you didn't murder someone, *but* Jesus took it even further than the Ten Commandments and said that if you hold anger in your heart toward someone, that is just as bad! *Wow!*
3. *Sin separates us from God* (see Rom. 6:23a).

4. *God loved us so much that He made a way for us to not remain separated from Him!* He sent His only Son, Jesus, to die on the cross for our sins. He paid the price for sin that we couldn't pay (see John 3:16).

5. *Jesus didn't stay dead but rose again, conquering sin and death.*

6. *Jesus is the only way to be saved* (see John 14:6). There are many people who believe in many different gods, but there is only one *true* God. You cannot be saved by being good enough, going to church enough or by helping lots of people. These are all good things, but they cannot save you from your sin. Even the very best that any person can do is still like dirty rags compared to God's holiness and perfection (see Isa. 64:6). Jesus is the only way to be saved!

7. *The Bible says that if you confess with your mouth that Jesus is Lord and believe in your heart that God raised Him from the dead, you will be saved* (see Rom. 10:9-10).

Creative Ways to Share the Gospel with Children

There are many creative ways to effectively share the gospel with children. There are also many tools you can use to help children understand, remember and apply the important message you are sharing. Visual aids, such as object lessons, illusions and props, as well as storytelling, help hold the attention of children and focus their thoughts. Using elements from your local culture, and finding ways to appeal to different learning styles, can all have a dramatic impact on how children connect to the message. Here are a few examples that will hopefully spark some ideas for your church's children's ministry!

Illusions

There are many illusions available online or at local magic stores that can be used to illustrate the gospel. Our favorite illusion that is easy to use and very powerful for all ages is the Cross Trick (www.crosstrick.com). We use it in most of our outreach events as well as in church service settings. The effect: a cup of clean water gets dirty when red "sin" is added. More clean water is added but it does not clear the water. The cross is presented, and when put in the water and stirred, the water becomes clear again.

Here is what you could say:

Boys and girls, I am really thirsty! (*Pour some water from a water bottle into a clear cup, leaving some water in the bottle.*) Does anyone want a drink? You know what? This water reminds me of our lives. In the beginning, the Bible records how God created *everything*. And He created the first two people, Adam and Eve. Their lives were just like this water, clean and pure. They had a friendship with God and walked and talked with Him. They were created in His image. But in order to have a true friendship, God gave them a choice—to obey what God said, or to do their own thing and ignore what God wanted. The Bible says that Adam and Eve decided to do their own thing and disobey God (*add red iodine to water*). Does anyone want a drink now? That's nasty! You see, this is what sin does to our lives—it messes it up. Sin is disobeying God—lying, stealing, disobeying our parents, wanting something that doesn't belong to us, even holding anger in our hearts toward someone. Boys and girls, sin separates us from God! That is a *big deal!* And the problem is that the Bible says in Romans 3:23 that *everyone* has sinned! That means that everyone has disobeyed God and is separated from Him! Not good. So some people think, "Well, I will be a good person" (*add a little more water*), or "I will go to church" (*add a little more water*), or "I will help others" (*add a little more water*). Are those things taking care of the sin? (*water is still red and nasty*) Those are good things, but they will not save you from your sin. But the good news is that God loved us so much that He made a way for us so that we wouldn't have to stay separated from Him forever. (*Hold up the cross.*) He sent His Son, Jesus, to die on the cross for our sins and pay a price that we could not pay on our own. Jesus said, "I am the way, the truth and the life, no one comes to the Father except through me" (John 14:6). (*Put cross in water and stir—water will become clear again.*) You see, Jesus is the *only* way to be saved! He is the *only* one that can take care of the sin in your life that separates you from God. You have a choice to make. The Bible says that the wages, or the cost, of sin is death, but the gift of God is eternal life through Jesus Christ. If you confess that Jesus is Lord and believe in your heart that God raised Him from the dead, you will be saved! If you are here today and would like to receive the payment that Jesus made for you, and begin a friendship with God today, please pray this with me: "Thank You, Jesus, that You died on the cross for my sins. I believe that You rose again from the dead. Please forgive me of my sins. I want to live the rest of my life for You. Thank You for saving me. Amen."

Object Lessons

Free Gift

For this object lesson, you need a brightly colored, wrapped box with a big bow and some candy or prize inside. You will use this prop to teach children that salvation is a free gift from God and that we don't have to do anything to earn it. All we have to do is accept it by faith.

Here is what you could say:

Who loves to get presents on your birthday or at Christmas? Raise your hand if you want to tell us in 10 seconds or less what your favorite birthday present was that you've ever received. (*Let a couple of kids tell about their favorite present.*) Who would like a present? Okay, Conner, come up front. (*Hand the child the gift, but tell him or her not to open it yet*) If I give you this gift as an early birthday present, how much would you have to pay for it? How many times would you have to clean your room? Would you have to do anything to earn it? No! Just receive it, because it's a gift. The person giving you a birthday gift has already paid for it! If I give this to you, will you just set it aside and never think about it again? No, you would be excited and open it! What if I told you that it was an iPad with your name engraved on it? What if you didn't believe me? Then you might not want it or maybe you wouldn't even open it. If you knew the gift was *free* and you believed that it was an iPad, then what would you do? Would you ask me how much money you need to raise to buy it? No, you would get excited and tear off the wrapping paper. You just helped to teach all of these kids an important lesson! (*Let the volunteer child open the present to keep.*)

Boys and girls, Conner just reminded me of something. Jesus has a free gift for us; He has already paid for it, so we don't have to do anything to earn it, and it's the *best* gift that anyone could *ever* receive! We just have to believe Him by faith and receive it! Some people choose not to believe, others believe but do not want to receive the gift. You can choose to believe God and His Word and receive this gift today!

It is the gift of salvation! God sent His only Son to die on the cross to pay the price for your sins. Sin is anything you do that is bad and goes against what the Bible says, like disobeying your parents, cheating on a test at school, holding anger in your heart toward someone, telling a lie. The Bible says that everyone has sinne, (see Rom. 3:23), even your mom or dad or pastor or teacher. The good news is that when Jesus died on the cross, He made a way for us to not stay separated from Him. After three days, Jesus rose again; He came back to life and now is in heaven with God. Jesus offers us the gift of eternal life. This means that one day when we die, we can go to heaven and live with Jesus forever! This is the best gift we can ever receive. In Romans 10:9-10, we read that if we believe in our hearts and confess with our mouths that Jesus is Lord, we will be saved! Who would like to pray with me to accept this free gift that is offered to us?

Adoption as Children of God

For this object lesson, all you need is a pet dog or cat! If you don't have a pet, you could ask one of your children's leaders if he or she has a pet to bring.

We had a birthday party for our dog Charlie at church for this illustration! A few weeks before, we advertised to the kids that we were having a birthday party for our dog Charlie and they were all invited! The kids got so excited about going to Charlie's birthday party! We picked up a doggie cake for Charlie and also bought a sheet cake that said "Happy Birthday, Charlie" for the kids to eat. We put up some balloons and party decorations. At the party, we had a lesson: "Boys and girls, this is Charlie, and he is my son. I know that you think he looks just like me: a brown beard, two eyes—but the truth is that he was not born as my son! Ms. Crystal didn't give birth to him! We adopted him into our family. When we did that, we became his parents. And we promised from that day on that we would love him, provide for his needs (food, a house, bed, toys), play with him, and never leave him on his own. He will always be a part of our family.

Here is what you could say:

Boys and girls, God did the same thing for us! God loved us so much that He provided a way for us to become a part of His family. The Bible says that everyone has sinned (see Rom. 3:23) and sin separates us from God. But God sent His Son, Jesus, to die for our sins (see John 3:16). Anyone who confesses that Jesus is Lord and believes in his or her heart that God raised Him from the dead will be saved! When we get saved, we become sons and daughters of God. He becomes our heavenly Father who loves us more than any person can ever love us. He promises to provide the things we need in our life. And He promises to never leave us! That is pretty awesome, isn't it?!

Stories

One powerful way to share the gospel is to use a dramatic story of a wrong-doing committed by one child to another, and then a severe punishment that follows. It is great to have some children from the audience come up and act it out as you tell the story. Once the punishment for the "offender" is stated, the other child (who was hurt by the offender) comes forward to take the punishment. At this point, the story moves from a fun story to a serious impact when it is related to what Jesus did for us! When using this type of story as an illustration with children, it's important to use elements that are understandable and relevant to them.

Here is what you could say:

I need two kids to help me out. Let's see, how about Jacob and Abby. They are going to be the characters in our story. One day at school, during lunch, Abby was working on her homework assignment. Jacob asked to borrow her iPad while she studied because he was bored. Later that day, some police officers—I need some police officers to help me out—came to the class and told the teacher that Abby had to come with them. She didn't know what to do. Why would they be asking for her? She quickly became afraid. The officers took her into the hall and told her that they had tracked illegal downloading of music and videos to her iPad. As Abby was trying to figure out what was happening, the teacher came up and told the police officers that she saw Jacob earlier downloading something on Abby's iPad during lunch. Jacob admitted that he used Abby's iPad to download those things. The officers told him that what he did was illegal and he was going to have to pay a $50,000 fine or else he would have to go to a juvenile detention center for one whole year—away from his friends and family! Jacob began to cry because he knew there was no way that he or his family could pay that much money. He didn't want to be taken away from his family for an entire year! *Wow*, boys and girls, that is a *crazy* punishment! Just as the police officers were about to take Jacob away, Abby came to them and said *"Wait!"* As they stopped and looked at her, she said "I will take the punishment for Jacob. I will go away from my family and friends for one year as punishment so that Jacob doesn't have to." Whoa. Boys and girls, would you do that for someone who did that to you? Jacob and Abby are teaching us an important lesson today. You see, Jesus paid the *ultimate* price for us that we couldn't pay for ourselves. The Bible says in Romans 6:23 that the cost of sin is *death*. Not just physical death, but spiritual death too—being separated from God forever. And the problem is that Romans 3:23 says that *everyone* has sinned. There is nothing you can do to pay for your sin—you can't be good enough; you can't go to church enough; you can't help enough people. But the great news is that God loved us so much that He made a way that we wouldn't have to stay separated from Him. He sent His Son, Jesus, to die on the cross and pay the price for our sins. And He didn't stay dead, but He rose again, conquering sin and death. And the Bible says that if you ask Jesus to be the Lord of your life and believe that God raised Him from the dead—you will be saved!

The Altar Call

Just like sunscreen, a biblical message is not effective in someone's life unless it is applied. I can sit in the sun, my sunscreen beside me, yet take no action in applying it to my body. The result is a red, crispy man, trying to figure out what happened! When we share the gospel with children, it is important to give an opportunity for them to respond to and apply the message to their lives. The altar call is simply an opportunity given to connect with children who want to respond to the good news they have just heard, and give their lives to Jesus. This can happen by asking the children who want to make a decision to accept Jesus as Lord to get out of their seats and talk with and pray with a children's ministry leader.

We usually ask the leaders to come line up across the front of the stage after the message, and then ask the children to come pray with one of the leaders. In the background, we play some quiet worship music and ask the children who stay at their seats to be respectful of the children coming up front by sitting quietly and praying for them from their seats. This action step of coming up and praying with the leaders helps with a few things. First, it helps the children understand that they have to *do* something. Romans 10:9-10 doesn't say we just need to believe in Jesus, but that we need to confess Him as Lord. Second, knowing who responded helps us as ministers connect with the children to help get them plugged in to the local church. We want to help them begin a journey of discipleship and growth, and get involved serving in ministry. After all, in the simplest terms, that is what ministers do—make disciples (see Matt. 28:19) and prepare the Body for works of service (see Eph. 4:12).

We have found that a powerful element in an altar call is training the children's ministry team to get involved with talking to and praying with the children. It gives them a chance to be a part of the exciting things God does in the children's lives. Also, some kids may connect with different leaders better. And, of course, not every child who comes forward during an altar call will be responding to the same thing. Some may want a leader to pray for their cat Muffin, or for a grandmother who is sick, or they may want to ask directions to the bathroom. A group of trained leaders can pray for the various needs, but also with those who want to respond to the gospel. They can also follow up with the children to make sure they have a Bible; they can send a postcard to celebrate one more time, and also keep you updated on the variety of needs and exciting testimonies of what God is doing in the children's ministry!

What Now?

It is exciting when a child responds to a salvation message! Now we want to give them the next steps to learn how to grow as a new child of God and as a Christian. "Grow in the grace and knowledge of our Lord and Savior Jesus Christ" (2 Pet. 3:18). If you plant a new plant and are excited about it, but you never water it or give it what it needs to grow, it won't do very well. When a child comes to Christ, we need to give him/her the right tools to grow. Here are some steps you can review with children who give their lives to Jesus. We usually take a few minutes after an altar call to briefly touch on these things. It helps them start thinking about it, and then you can follow up in more detail with parents or through a teaching series.

"Boys and girls, if you asked Jesus to save you and come into your life, the Bible says you are now a new person! Your sins are forgiven and you now have a friendship with Jesus! Here are a few things that will help you start growing as a child of God."

1. *Read the Bible.* "The Bible is God's Word and teaches us about God's promises for His children. The Bible is where we learn about who God is and what He is like, and how we should live our lives as a Christian. If you don't have a Bible, we can get one to you today. Begin reading it every day. If you don't know how to read, you can have your mom or dad, brother or sister, help read to you. A good place to start is the book of John." (We keep Bibles on hand, in a translation that is easy to understand, for children who do not have a Bible available to them.)

2. *Pray.* "Praying is simply talking to and listening to God. You don't have to use any special words; you can just talk to Him like you would talk to a friend. You are building a relationship with God when you pray."

Prayer Object Lesson—Here is an object lesson that can be used while talking about prayer. All you need is a cell phone, or for even more impact, use a giant inflatable phone.

"How many of you have a best friend? Do you ever talk to him or her?" (*Have a child volunteer come up to the front of the room. Give the child a phone, and you will have a big phone. Then proceed to pretend to call the child. Tell the kids that you are pretending that the child up front is your best friend. Keep pretending to call, and each time you call, quickly ask for all sorts of random stuff—you need someone to do your chores for you; your cat is sick and needs someone to take care of it; you need to borrow something; and so on. Do not give the child a chance to say much; just make your request and hang up. Call over and over, asking for lots of stuff and not listening.*) Say, "Am I being a good friend? No! Why? That's right, because I am only calling when I need something. And

I do all of the talking and don't give time to listen to my friend talk to me. Boys and girls, many people do that to God. They only want to talk to Him when they need something, and they never spend any time listening to God. Jesus wants to be our best friend. It is okay to ask for things that we need, because He cares about us very much. But we also want to talk to Him about other things too—like how thankful we are for what He has done for us; how much we love Him; and things that we talk to other friends about. Praying is simply talking to God and listening to God. And you can talk to God anytime! He doesn't have to go home like your other friends. He is always with you—even on weekends and holidays!"

3. *He will never leave you!* (See Deut. 31:6 and Matt. 28:20.) "When you asked Jesus to come into your life, the Bible says that the Holy Spirit came to live in you! He is always with you and promises to never leave you alone."

4. *Go to church.* "It is healthy to go to church regularly because it is a place where you get to meet together with other Christians, worship God together, encourage each other, help each other and learn more about God together" (see Heb. 10:25).

5. *Share the Good News with others.* "God just changed your life *forever*! That is great news! You can start sharing that good news with others today. You can tell your parents, brothers, sisters, grandparents, neighbors, kids at your school, kids on your bus, everywhere you go what Jesus did for you—that He forgave your sins and became your best friend. God wants to use you to share His love with others and help them come to know Jesus too."

6. *Get baptized in water.* "Jesus wants everyone who believes in Him to be baptized in water. Baptism doesn't save you, but it shows everyone on the outside what Jesus did on the inside of you. If someone looks at you, will they be able to see Jesus in your heart? What if a doctor opens up your heart and looks in, will he or she be able to see Jesus in there? No. Your life is different now, but baptism is a way to tell everyone what Jesus did in your life. What is a symbol or

a sign? That's right, something that points to or shows something else. The sign is not the thing, right? Like an ice cream shop sign isn't actually made out of ice cream, but it tells you that inside there is real ice cream you can eat! Romans 6:3-4 says that baptism is a symbol of us dying with Jesus (going under water, dying to sin and our old life), and being raised again to new life with Him (coming back out of the water as a new person)."

Teaching Children to Share the Gospel

True discipleship happens when someone receives Jesus as the Lord of his or her life, begins to grow, and starts reaching people for Jesus and helping them grow. As children's evangelist John Tasch says, "Children are never too young to do something great for God!" After children give their life to Jesus, it is the perfect time to teach them that God wants to use them to tell others about Jesus as well and share the good news. They are not too young to do something great for God. If they learn how to share their faith at a young age, when they are older, it will be a common part of their life (which is how it should be).

One way that we have done this is by teaching kids in simple terms how to explain the gospel and pray with someone. We also teach them a simple prayer that we repeat over and over again so they can memorize it. "Thank You, Jesus, that You died on the cross for my sins. I believe that You rose again from the dead. Please forgive me of my sins and come into my life. I want to live the rest of my life for You. Thank You for saving me. Amen."

A fun way for the children to practice this is by having them come up and role-play. One child can volunteer to not know anything about Jesus, and another child volunteers to talk to the first child about what Jesus did for him or her, and why he/she needs Him. One time, we were trying to come up with a creative way to do this when we realized that one of our main puppet characters, Rupert, had never accepted Christ in front of the children. So we decided that it would be fun to have the children lead him to Christ. We had an eight-year-old girl in our children's ministry come up and talk to him. Rupert told her that he didn't know Jesus. So she told him all about Jesus and what He did for us. She asked Rupert if he wanted to pray with her to ask Jesus in his heart. She then prayed with him in front of all the kids. All the kids love this puppet character, and they were so excited for him.

This showed the kids how simple it is to tell people about Jesus and lead them to Christ. We also told the kids that they are never too young to tell someone about Jesus. We encouraged them to tell their friends and then come back the next week and tell us about it. We had kids come back and tell us about their experiences and then we talked about them with all the kids. Most of them came back so excited to know that they were able to lead someone to Christ.

One little girl, about six years old, came back the next week very sad. She told us that she talked to a friend at school about Jesus. Her friend said that she did not want to accept Christ. The little girl was very discouraged. We used this time as a teaching moment for all the kids. We told them that Jesus wants us to share the gospel, and that's our responsibility. Not everyone will accept it or believe us, but we can't let that stop us from talking about it. We also encouraged her by letting her know that even though her friend told her no, she still may think about it. We can pray that the Holy Spirit will help her remember what they had talked about. We celebrated that this little girl had shared the gospel, and we told her how proud we were of her.

Here is an object lesson about sharing the gospel: Take a big pack of gum or candy. Start walking around the room with it and offering it to children. "Would you like a piece of gum?" Most of the kids will say yes; some may say, "No, thank you." As you are doing this, stop at a couple of kids and say out loud to yourself, "Hmm, I'm not sure if I should offer him a piece. I'm scared he might say no. He may be mad or not like me anymore if I offer him a piece." Then the kids will start shouting at you that he will probably say yes. Use this object lesson to teach kids how easy it is to share the gospel with other kids. Ask the kids who said yes to the gum if they were glad that you offered it to them. "Think about the person who told you about Jesus; are you glad that person told you? Aren't you glad he or she didn't get too scared and not say anything to you? Think of this when you are telling others. Jesus tells us in Mark 16:15 (*NLT*) to 'Go into all the world and preach the Good News to everyone, everywhere.'"

It is so exciting to watch children respond to the gospel and be changed by the power of the Holy Spirit! And it is an honor to be a part of that process by sharing the gospel with them. Pray that the Holy Spirit will give you and your team creative ways to share the gospel. He will also help you as you go out and talk to people. As you preach the gospel to the young lives that God has brought across your path, remember to give them an opportunity to respond. We never know what the Holy Spirit is doing in a child's life, whether he or she is a visitor or a regular church member. God's Word is powerful, and as we preach it, it will not return to Him without effect (see Isa. 55:11). Keep up the great work!

DISCUSSION QUESTIONS

1. What is one idea from this chapter we can implement this week at our next service or outreach?
2. Are we presenting the gospel to the children on a regular basis?
3. Are we including the essential elements of the gospel, or are there important things we are leaving out to be simple or quick? Name the elements of the gospel that are essential to cover.
4. Are we teaching the kids how to present the gospel? Practice presenting the gospel with each other the way you would teach the children to share it with others. What are some creative ways that we can teach children to share the gospel with their friends?
5. What are some good Scriptures to memorize and use when presenting the gospel to children?
6. Have we talked to the kids about the steps they can take, after they accept Jesus, to grow as a Christian?
7. What props or illustrations can we use this month to help illustrate the gospel? What are some cultural things we can use for illustrations that the children in our area would connect to? What are some other objects or stories we can use to present the gospel?
8. How can we present the gospel to appeal to different learning styles (i.e., visual, auditory, physical, and so on)?
9. Are we using church lingo or phrases that may be confusing for the children when we are talking to them about the gospel (e.g., "covered in the blood of the Lamb")?
10. What other leaders and volunteers are involved in praying with children and presenting the gospel besides the children's pastor?

11. Team Game: Get a box of objects and pass them out to each person or small group. Give everyone five minutes to think of a creative illustration to use that object to present the gospel. Give a prize for the most creative idea! After you come up with an object lesson, use this chapter to review and see if you included all of the essential elements of the gospel in your presentation.

11

Training Volunteers to Share the Gospel with Confidence

JIM WIDEMAN

Jim Wideman is considered an innovator, pioneer and one of the fathers of the modern children's ministry movement. He is a speaker, teacher, author, leadership coach, and ministry consultant, with more than 35 years of hands-on experience in the local church. Jim has trained hundreds of thousands of children's and student ministry leaders from all denominations and sizes of congregations around the world. In the 1980s, the International Network of Children's Ministry (INCM) awarded him with their "Ministry of Excellence Award"; in the '90s, *Children's Ministry Magazine* named him one of the 10 Pioneers of the Decade; in 2010, *Children's Ministry Magazine* once again named him one of the 20 Top Influencers in Children's Ministry;

and in 2012, the INCM presented him with their first ever Legacy Award for his lifetime achievement in children's ministry. Jim currently oversees all the Next Generation and Family Ministries, birth through college, at World Outreach Church in Murfreesboro, Tennessee. Jim and his amazing wife, Julie, have two successful daughters, two handsome sons-in-law, and the cutest grandson ever born!

Twitter: @jimwideman
Facebook /jimwidemanministries
Blog: jimwideman.blogspot.com
Instagram: jimwideman
Website: www.jimwideman.com

I had no idea that saying yes to the command "Get your guitar and your Bible and go back to children's church" from my pastor, in 1977, would change my life forever. Not only has it changed me as a person and Christ follower, but it has also changed me as a husband, father, employee and minister; and it has changed the lens through which I view everything. It began a journey that, at 58 years young and counting, I'm still on—to know God and love His Word and help sons and daughters do the same.

I've told this story for years, but it bears repeating for the reader who has never heard it. I had been working with teenagers for three years, serving in churches and playing in a Christian rock 'n' roll band when my pastor came looking for me and told me to go cover children's church for the teacher who called in last minute and informed him she was not coming back. I wanted to help my pastor, so I did what he said.

I grabbed my guitar and Bible and I went back to the old fellowship hall with seven kids. *How hard could this be?* I thought. The answer came just minutes into the hour and a half that turned into a month all in one day. It was the hardest thing I had ever done on short notice. I was not prepared, and the kids could smell the fresh blood just like a group of sharks. They ate me up!

I went to find my pastor as soon as the last child had been picked up, and I wanted to know how long I was going to have to do this. I'll never forget Brother Wilson's reply to me: "You'll need to do it until God raises up someone with a vision." Immediately, I began to pray, *Lord, give someone a vision for children's ministry! Open their eyes, Lord, and let them see the importance of reaching and teaching kids from Your viewpoint!*

After praying that prayer and working with the children over the next several weeks, I soon realized that I was that someone Jesus had given the vision to. How did I come to this realization? I had begun to see children's ministry from a different viewpoint—a biblical viewpoint, a gospel viewpoint. For the first time ever as a young Christ follower, I began to see that children and the importance of ministering to them were not only in the Bible but that every child needs the gospel, the good news that Jesus is the one and only Son of God. He is the only way that anyone can be saved. He is the only way to the Father, and everyone young and old needs to know this.

This is what we exist for—to make Jesus known. Jesus died on the cross for the sins of mankind; but death could not hold Him. On the third day, the same Holy Spirit that lives in you and me raised Christ Jesus from the dead.

He's alive and sits at the right hand of God, making intercession for the saints (us). Every child needs this gospel.

The Bible is the benchmark for how we should view the world and how we live. My goal for every child I have the opportunity to teach and pastor is for him or her to grow up to become a doer of the Word. I realized early in my ministry that children couldn't live what they couldn't remember, and they couldn't remember what they didn't understand. It changed the way I taught, the methods I used and how visual and simple I needed to communicate; but most of all, they needed a model or example. Show is needed along with tell!

You and I are the only examples of being a doer of the Word that some children will ever see. I want to give and live the gospel to every child I have the honor of teaching. There are lots of voices that speak into their lives that challenge the message of the gospel. As a parent, and as a pastor, I cannot block out every voice that speaks to my family and to my congregation, nor should I; but I have spent my life pointing out that God's Word contains truth, and the truth of the Word is what will set us free. God's Word is the filter we should view the world through!

As teachers, we have to look for every opportunity to correct the voices children feed on with the voice of the gospel. Years ago, I learned that all a stronghold is, is believing wrong information. Our job is not to entertain children or creatively fill the time we have with them at church. Our job is to give them the gospel and share it with confidence so that strongholds can be demolished. With this in mind, here's how I train my volunteers to share the gospel with confidence.

You Can't Give Away What You Don't Have

I require every person in our ministry to know Christ. (It will really help your ministry to know Christ!) As a part of our worker application, we ask folks to write their God story. We want to know not only about their redemption story; we also want to know about their walk. All of us who minister to children should have a God story. We also encourage folks to share their "Yay, God!" stories, in and out of the classroom, all the time. I start every meeting with listening to God stories. The more our volunteers get in the habit of freely sharing their God stories, the more it becomes a way of life. I like to ask people this question: "Has there ever been a time when you were more in love with

Jesus than you are right now?" If the answer is yes, I tell that person that he or she is the only one who can do something about it.

Model What You Want Children to Become

What you model for children to do now will follow them into adulthood. Never forget that when it comes to Bible living, when you point at others there are three fingers pointing back at you. There can't be one set of rules for you and another set for them. Follow Paul's words: "Come follow me as I follow Christ" (see 1 Cor. 11:1). I ask that all volunteers be baptized in water and live a separated life. I ask for references so that I can confirm their walk with the Lord.

Make a list of everything you want children to become spiritually—givers, prayer warriors, doers of the Word—and put examples of all those things before them. At the beginning of every new school year, we review with our leaders our goals for every student. If you aim at nothing, you hit it every time. Here's what we want every volunteer to aim at as they teach so that every child has the following opportunities:

- Know who God is
- Know who Jesus is
- Develop a love and respect for God's Word, the Bible
- Know the purpose of the cross
- Receive Jesus as their personal Savior
- Participate in water baptism
- Be introduced to and cooperate with the Holy Spirit
- Have a heart to pray, serve and give to God's work at home and all around the world
- Desire God's plan and purposes for their lives

Teach Principles

The number one mistake in teaching the Bible to children is to fill them with facts instead of instilling in them the principles of each story and teaching. Facts go in our heads, while principles go in our hearts and help us walk out the truths within. Kids need the principles of the Word to apply to their everyday life. Do the children you teach understand the principles within the stories, or do they just know the stories?

Teach the Value of Wisdom

Let children know that wisdom is better than money or fame. One of the greatest lessons I ever learned is that the voice of wisdom and the voice of God are always the same thing. That's why I need to know God's Word, because it also contains His wisdom. The world tells kids that life is about fame and fortune. I know parents who are more concerned with their child's ability to produce wealth than to instill the pursuit of wisdom and God's truth above all else. The Bible says that wisdom is better than riches or gold. If someone is wise, that wisdom will bring blessing, honor and a good name. Knowledge is the beginning of wisdom. God's wisdom brings blessings. Look for every opportunity to point out godly wisdom in every lesson. Pointing out God's wisdom in every story or lesson brings eternal results.

Teach the Infallibility of God's Word

Teach children that whatever the answer they are looking for is found in God's Word. How should we treat others? Who should we forgive? Who should we be friends with? How should we treat our parents, our family and our employer? Who should we vote for? What should our nation's views on Israel be? It's all in the Book! The wisdom of the Bible is not just for Sunday and Wednesday; it's also for Monday, Tuesday, Thursday, Friday and Saturday. This is the guidebook on living and the filter through which every voice should be listened. God's Word is not outdated; it's relevant for today!

One of the things you can do with your children, both at home and at church, is to gather the questions kids are asking and give them the answers from God's Word. I look for every opportunity to give chapter and verse to the questions they are facing. When you're answering their questions, make sure you tell them what Jesus did. Don't wait for them to ask; include it in how you teach. Every time Jesus faced the devil or demonic opposition, He spoke the Word. Our tongue has the power of life and death. So when we speak the Word, we speak words of life

As parents and pastors, we need to help kids watch their words and be intentional about saying what the Word says. This is also how we build our faith. Faith comes by hearing. When we say God's Word, it pumps us up and builds our faith like reps with dumbbells and barbells. What confessions should you lead your children in to get God's Word in their hearts? I love getting children to speak God's Word as a way of learning the Word. We don't live by bread alone but by every word that comes from God.

Look for Teachable Moments

Guiding young people to take those first steps toward faith can be the most rewarding opportunity of life for both parents and teachers. The journey toward faith is filled with teachable moments when influential adults and peers answer questions, teach biblical truths, model Christian values, and share personal testimonies that further the student's understanding. When talking to a student about salvation, follow these helpful steps:

- *Ask follow-up questions.* When a student asks a question, often he or she does not know exactly what to ask. Get clarification before deciding how to answer a question. For example, you might say, "Tell me more about what you are thinking." Or "What made you ask that question? Where did you hear about this?" Remember, many times the question a student asks may not be the actual question for which he/she is needing an answer. Avoid asking questions that can be answered with yes or no.
- *Avoid giving more information than a student needs.* Adults can be tempted to tell all they know on a subject. When a student asks a question, only answer what the student is asking. If a student asks for more information, be more specific with your answers.
- *Don't jump to conclusions.* A student may ask, "Why did Andy get baptized?" This question may be a request only for information, not a request for the gospel presentation. If they want more, then give them the gospel.
- *Speak in clear terms.* Avoid symbolic analogies that may distract from discussion and understanding. Speak English, not church-ese.

- *Use simple wording.* Rather than using the phrase "accepting Jesus into your heart," say the words "becoming a Christian" or "becoming a Christ follower."

Look for Opportunities to Share the Gospel with Children

Here are some simple steps I teach my volunteers to use to talk to students about the plan of salvation:

1. *God loves you and has great plans for you* (see. Ps 139:13-16). Talk about these truths: God made people; God made you. God wants to have a relationship with people, and God wants to have a relationship with you. Say, "Tell me one way you know God loves you."

2. *We have all sinned* (see Rom. 3:23). Everyone must understand that he/she is separated from God. Sin is best understood as choosing to do things our own way instead of God's way. (Give some examples of sin, such as disobedience, ungratefulness, untruthfulness, and the like.) Then ask the student, "Have you sinned? What does God think about sin?" Point out that everyone has sinned.

3. *Even though we choose to sin, God still loves us and offers to forgive us* (see Rom. 5:8). Ask, "How do you think it makes God feel when you sin?" Focus on the fact that God loves the student even when he or she sins. Say, "God promised that one day a Savior would come and not sin and would die for all people. Do you know who that Savior is? Did you know that He died for you?"

4. *Jesus died for us* (see John 3:16). Talk about John 3:16 and explain that because sin separates people from God, everyone needs a Savior. Ask, "Do you know why Jesus died?" Say, "Jesus loved you so much that He willingly died for you so that you could be with God forever." If the student is old enough to understand the resurrection, say, "Jesus rose from the dead so that we could have eternal life."

5. *You can become a Christian by confessing that Jesus is your Savior and Lord* (see Rom. 10:9). Ask, "Would you like to be a Christian?" The

word "confess" in this verse means that you say that Jesus is your Savior and that you must:

- **A**dmit that you have sinned.
- **B**elieve that Jesus is God's Son.
- **C**onfess that Jesus is Savior and Lord.

6. *Review and follow up.* Encourage a student to tell you in his or her own words what he or she understands and believes. Either ask the student to repeat a prayer after you or help the student know what to say in his or her prayer. Read Romans 10:13 and remind the student that this verse is a promise. Jesus will be his or her Savior forever.

Partner with Parents

Make sure that you share with parents about your conversations with their child. Let the child tell the parents what his or her decision was for the Lord and His Word. Also make sure you report this good news to your coordinator or leader so they can follow up with parents and children about their next steps.

Back in 2008, I wrote an article in *KidzMatter Magazine* entitled "Leading with Help." In that article, I talked about how it is not God's plan for us to do ministry or life alone; that is why He sent us the Holy Spirit. The Holy Spirit is our teacher, our guide, our helper and our comforter! When the pressures and problems of teaching kids and leading others come, you don't need to try to handle them in your own strength, but in the strength and power of the Spirit of the living God!

Just because you are doing the Lord's work doesn't mean you won't have problems. We all have problems. Psalm 34:19 tells us, "A righteous man may have many troubles, but the Lord delivers him from them all" (Ps. 34:19); 2 Corinthians 4:8-9 says, "We are hard pressed on every side, but not crushed; perplexed, but not in despair; persecuted, but not abandoned; struck down, but not destroyed" (2 Cor. 4:8-9). I believe this verse describes us as getting-up people! When we lead with the help of our helper the Holy Spirit, we are not leading in our own strength but in the strength of the promised power source. This also works with teaching.

In that article, I talked about a very valuable lesson I learned several years ago about relying on my Helper. One day, as I was leaving for work, I had an impression in my spirit that I needed to bring my bass guitar with me to church. Rather than be quick to obey, I started reasoning with myself. To make a long story short, I blew off the leading and went to work. No sooner had I walked in my office than the phone rang. It was my Wednesday night bass player in my pre-youth class informing me that he just got to work and found out he had to work late and asked if I could play bass for him. My Helper (the Holy Spirit) had wanted to help me save time.

As I drove back home to get my bass, I saw that the more I listened to the voice of the Spirit in small things, the easier it was to hear Him in major decisions. I also realized that it would have been better for me to bring my bass and not need it than to blow off the voice of the Spirit. I've also learned through the years to never disobey a check in my spirit. If I sense a strong leading to not go somewhere or to not do something or to pass on a worker even if I can't explain it, I trust my Helper. Not only can the Holy Spirit help you in leading the children's ministry, but also we must help our teachers and volunteer workforce learn to live the Spirit-led life in and out of the classroom.

If we want children to be led by the Spirit, we must model it! Here are 10 practical ways we can encourage others and ourselves to be led by the Spirit in children's ministry:

1. Start early in the week inviting your Helper to help you. Get in the habit of reading next week's lesson when you get home from church, and ask the Holy Spirit to guide you this next week to make it real to the children. Go ahead and highlight key areas that jump out at you.

2. Pray for the children as the Spirit guides you! Call out their name and pray what flows from your heart for each child and his or her family. Repeat this step throughout the week. Also pray that you are sensitive to where each student is spiritually. Ask the Lord to show you places where you can share the gospel, as well as pray for the needs the students have during the class time.

3. Set an appointment to plan and study your lesson. Start from the beginning, asking for the Spirit to guide your plans. Read the curriculum but listen to the Holy Spirit. I treat all curricula (even stuff

I write) like catfish. I let the Holy Spirit pick out the meat, and I leave the bones! Don't wait until the last minute to study. This is an important step! Never equate flowing with the Spirit to flying by the seat of your pants. I want to have enough time to obey what the Spirit says; some things my Helper has led me to must be ordered or purchased.

4. Come early and be prepared. I like to set up my classroom, my props and teaching tools ahead of time so I have time to pray before the kids arrive. I like to pray over every chair. Kids are creatures of habit, and many times they sit in the same area. So I call their names and let the Spirit guide me to stand in the gap for their needs and their families.

5. As the children arrive, let the Spirit direct how you spend your time. A common mistake I've seen with all the children's workers I've worked with is that they talk amongst themselves rather than allow the Spirit to guide the pre-service time, as well as the lesson. Also look for opportunities to talk with parents. Parents love to hear positive things about their children. Look for ways you can help parents be better parents. Ask about prayer requests and things that you, as a class, have been trusting God to do for that family.

6. Trust your Guide. I used to illustrate this in children's church by blindfolding a child and giving him or her verbal instructions to carry out without bumping into things. (It's impossible to walk by faith, not sight, in our own strength.) Then I would ask another child to come be a guide (just like the Holy Spirit is our guide) and guide the blindfolded child to safety. It's much easier with a guide to follow the Word of the Lord. I have found that practice makes perfect, not only in playing an instrument or developing a skill, but also in trusting our Guide! Don't beat yourself up if you miss an opportunity; we serve the God of the second chance!

7. During the lesson feel free to follow the Spirit's guide. I love video and other teaching aides, but the most important resource you can have in the classroom is a Spirit-led teacher! He or she knows how to follow the Spirit's leading and end up accomplishing the desired outcome for the corporate vision. Remember the goals for

each student we've already mentioned above. Let the Spirit guide you toward making these a reality in each student's life.

8. After class, don't be in a hurry to leave. Listen for the Spirit to guide your after-class time. In my experience, this has been when kids wait for others to leave, and they open up. Also be sensitive to follow up with parents and also carry out any other out-of-class ministry you should do this coming week. Remember, Jesus shared the gospel as He did life. He was sitting at a well when a lady came by. He asked her for a drink and then gave the whole salvation message by comparing it to the Living Water. This is why Jesus was a master teacher; He took everyday tasks and situations and used them to share the gospel. We need to develop that same skill.

9. After I minister and head out to attend a service, I rely on the help of the Holy Spirit to lead me to people I need to recruit to be on my team. I'm always asking the Holy Spirit to guide me to people who need to be needed! I'm on a mission from God to connect with those He leads me to. Jesus was out and about when He found the 12 disciples. The Holy Spirit is my number one recruiting tool. The best thing to use to talk to others is what Jesus is doing in the lives of the children. Be ready to share the God stories. People want to be a part of ministries and activities that get results. Be quick to testify what Jesus is doing in the lives of children and families. Also be sure to share the ways your life has been blessed because you have been willing to give the gospel to children.

10. Learn to allow the Spirit to help you identify things that need correcting or that need to be improved on a regular basis. Ask Him to teach you why it needs fixing as well as how. To me the Holy Spirit works in our lives like a spotlight. He shines or illuminates things that need to be changed. This is true in the classroom as well as every other area of my life! Evaluation is the key to the pursuit of excellence. Also ask the Holy Spirit to help you evaluate how you are doing with giving away the gospel. The Spirit will guide you to be the best teacher you can be. He is on your side. He wants God's best for your life.

The Holy Spirit is a safe guide who can always be trusted. The voice of wisdom and the voice of God are always the same thing. Our Helper, the Holy Spirit, will lead us to all truth and will never disagree with the voice of wisdom or God's words! One of my favorite verses is Proverbs 3:5-6: "Trust in the Lord with all your heart and lean not on your own understanding; in all your ways acknowledge him, and he will make your paths straight." This is also true in the classroom. I am so glad we have a Helper to lead us to be the leaders and teachers we need to be. Listen to your Guide. Your Helper is right beside you. Listen to Him, learn from Him and do what He says.

You are not alone in the awesome task of teaching and training children to be fully devoted follows of Christ now and forever. Every list of things that need to change starts with us desiring what God wants for us and for those we are ministering to. Desire to be led by the Spirit like never before. Model this to those who serve with you.

One of the best ways to encourage a certain kind of behavior in others is to be an example of that behavior and model it. Jesus modeled the Spirit-led life; He never ministered the same way to each person but was led my God's Spirit. It's good news to know that the same Spirit that led Jesus, the same Spirit that empowered Him and raised Him from the dead, lives and empowers us today. Thank God for our Helper!

These things don't happen without training. "Training" is one of the most misunderstood words used in the church world. Most church leader confuse the word "training" with verbal instruction. We have a little talk with folks and call it training. Nothing could be further from the truth. Ask anyone who has ever been trained outside the church and they'll tell you that training might begin with verbal instruction, but then it moves on to hands-on doing, gentle correction, further instruction and on-the-job learning. That's what training is all about.

That's also true in training others to share the gospel. I think we are guilty of dumping workers in a classroom rather than training them first. You will set up your new workers for success when you allow them to watch and learn over time rather than just dumping them in a classroom and saying, "Tag, you're it."

I don't know why it took me so long to grasp this practice, but as long as I have been working there has been a 90-day probation period for all new employees. One day, I asked myself why we take new ministry workers, have a little talk with them and then just throw them to the children. What if I established a probation period for volunteers and assigned them to a teacher to coach, mentor and show them what to do? So, we established a 30-day probation period where folks learned by watching and assisting. At the end of the 30 days, I would meet with them and see if where they were serving was a good fit. If not, I would begin the process again and assign them to a different area.

"Why, Jim?" you ask. It's simple. People won't last if they only have a job and don't feel they are a fit or have made a connection. In my book *Volunteers That Stick*, I called that establishing a volunteer career. This is very important. Now that the new recruit has found a home, he or she can begin to learn by doing. I encourage helpers to learn by doing small assignments. The Bible tells us to not despise small beginnings. Everyone has to start somewhere.

The Bible also lets us know that if we are faithful with small things, God will make us a ruler over more. That's how you help develop depth in your teaching team. Allow each person time to learn, time to ask questions. Allow time to get good at communicating the gospel, not just by doing it alone but with a coach to help him or her develop confidence. I love working as a team where we can offer suggestions to one another on how to improve our presentation of the gospel.

I believe that teaching children is not just a good thing to do. I believe it is God's work, and it is a matter of life and death—eternal life or eternal death. That's why we must work at developing our abilities to share the gospel with confidence. This only comes with practice. This only comes with work—with intentional, consistent behavior to pursue a desired outcome. "What desired outcome?" you ask. The reason we exist as children's ministers—for the spread of the gospel.

We are not program directors. We are not baby-sitters. We are not kid keepers. We're ministers. "But you are a chosen people, a royal priesthood, a holy nation, God's special possession, that you may declare the praises of him who called you out of darkness into his wonderful light" (1 Pet. 2:9). If believers are priests, what should we do? We should do the work of the ministry.

The most important thing that should be taking place in our children's classrooms is not just the teaching of material or the passing on of biblical knowledge. It's the good news of the gospel: "This gospel of the kingdom will be proclaimed throughout the world as a testimony to all the nations, and then the end will come" (Matt. 24:14, *ESV*). This is our mission!

DISCUSSION QUESTIONS

1. Get your team together and tell your redemption stories. Practice telling the stories in a way that is concise and simple to understand.
2. Who are some of the people God used to write your God stories? What sticks out to you about this person who made such an impact on you?
3. Of all the gospel presentations you have seen in a sermon or during class, which one was the most impactful to you? Why was it so effective?
4. List ways you want the children in your ministry to grow spiritually.
5. What is your favorite Bible story? What makes it your favorite?
6. This week, share the gospel with three people from three different age groups. Practice telling the gospel in a simple way each person can understand.
7. Discuss some ways that you could partner with parents better.
8. How can you allow the Holy Spirit to help you become better in your ministry?
9. What are your spiritual goals for every child in your ministry?
10. What can you do to train others more effectively? Write out an action plan.

12

Mom, Dad and Salvation

LARRY FOWLER

Larry Fowler's latest role in his storied 30-year ministry career is as executive director of global networking for Awana and KidzMatter. Larry travels the country connecting with churches and helping them build dynamic ministries to children, youth and families.

In 2012, the International Network of Children's Ministry (INCS) gave Larry its Legacy Award for 30 years of service in children's ministry. In his ministry career, Larry has served as a local-church Awana leader, missionary, speaker, author, teacher, pastor and executive director of international ministries, program development and training.

"Larry, I want to become a Christian." David, a sixth-grader, told me this at the end of the Sunday evening junior high group that I led as a very young, green youth pastor. I was thrilled—David was only the second person in my ministry to come to Christ. So right then and there I counseled him, and David trusted in Christ. His parents were strong believers and faithful attenders of our church, and I knew they would be really happy that their son was saved, and so I told him, "When you get home, you've got to tell your parents what you did tonight." *It never occurred to me to involve them in the decision.*

"Diane, I want to do that," eight-year-old Maggie whispered to my wife while they were sitting next to one another in a large-group time. Maggie was referring to what the special guest was talking about: She was sharing her testimony about how she had come to Christ. Diane knew Maggie's dad, and she knew that he would want to be there for the special moment. She whispered back, "Let's tell your dad as soon as he comes to get you. He'll want to help you." Maggie's dad was ecstatic and had the awesome privilege of leading his daughter to Christ that night because of Diane's wise direction. *She knew it was best to involve parents in their child's salvation decision.*

Trevor lingered after the other kids left and came up to the front to talk to me after the large-group time. "Mr. Larry, I'm not sure my sins are forgiven." I was a guest speaker, and my lesson had been on that topic. Trevor was thinking—deeply—about it. "Then, let's get your dad and we'll all talk together about that." As a more experienced children's worker, I knew it would be best to involve the parents. Though I was a guest, I also knew that Trevor's dad was a kidmin leader in a different age group. I figured he would be thrilled at Trevor's interest in the gospel. Thinking back later, I knew that at that moment I missed Trevor's body language: a downward look said he didn't want to include his dad; he just wanted to talk to me. But I was so focused on my plan that I said, "Let's find your dad," and took off with Trevor in tow.

Most people were leaving, and as I approached Trevor's dad, I saw his wife (who was not a worker) talking with him, so I waited to say something until they were finished. I missed another body language clue: Trevor's mom was in a hurry and had just told her husband so. I stepped up to Dad and pulled Trevor right beside me. "Mike," I said, "Trevor has some questions about salvation, and I thought you'd want to help me answer them for him." I never could have anticipated Mike's response: "Oh, he did that already. Come on, Trevor, we've got to go." He grabbed Trevor's hand and the two of them left—just like that. I was stunned at how quickly Mike dismissed the moment. As a guest, I never got to follow up; I often wondered if Mike took the time later to ask Trevor what his question was and help him get the answer he was seeking.

It took me too long in my children's ministry journey to recognize the importance of involving parents when their child is ready to trust Christ. As I've related above, Diane and I have had mixed experiences, some good, some not so good. The failed experience with Mike and Trevor pushed my resolve to not only involve parents, but to also *instruct* them. That is the focus of this chapter; our prayer is that in your role as a children's worker, you will consider this issue and grow in your understanding of it.

What Should We Do?

As children's workers, what *should* we do when a child wants to trust Christ as Savior? There are three levels of action to consider.

Responsibility #1: We Should Inform the Parents

When a child makes any spiritual decision, parents should be notified. Too often, though, we just don't. We either don't think about it, we don't have the parent information readily available, or we are just too busy. Guilty? If you admit that you are, then you have lots of company. I think the percentage of children's ministries that intentionally inform parents of a child's decision is unacceptably low.

Often, we rely on the child to do it. I've been in evangelism training that promotes the idea that when a child accepts Christ as Savior, he or she should go tell someone—especially a family member. In fact, if the child is from a Christian family, we were reminded to say, "Go tell your parents what you have just done." I think it would be better if we are *with* the child when the parents are told.

Doesn't it make sense that parents *should* know—whether they are Christian parents or not? We'll tell the parents about what craft the child made or what positive behaviors we observe; shouldn't we tell them about the most important decision their child is making?

"Parents *ought* to hear about it," you say, "but what if . . ." And you go on to reveal your hesitation. Here are some I've heard:

Objection #1
Unbelieving parents may not want us talking to their children about spiritual decisions. *Then we should clarify our intention with them up front.* Do you have a permission statement as part of your child registration? I recommend you include wording such as this:

> In _____ (your program's name), volunteers regularly challenge children to consider spiritual issues and encourage them to make personal decisions concerning their own faith. I give my permission for my child, if he or she so desires, to be included in those discussions. I understand that I am welcome to observe at any time and can ask for further information on any topic that is taught to my child.

In my experience, this is an objection that is overblown. Generally, parents want their children to think through spiritual issues, and they support their children learning about God—even when they themselves don't want to.

Objection #2
There's no time or opportunity. *"Things are really hectic when the parents pick up their kids, and everyone is so busy."* If that's what you are thinking, you need to make time.

I recently met Kevin Harper. He's the children's pastor at Journey Church in Edmond, Oklahoma, and he attended a tour event for mega churches that I hosted. It started the day after Easter, and I noticed that as we were eating and getting acquainted, he was spending a lot of time on the phone. *I hope he isn't dealing with some big crisis,* I thought. The next day he told the group in a networking time what he was doing: "On Easter weekend," he said, "we had about 200 children indicate they wanted to accept Christ. We have a policy that the parents of every single child who responds get a call from us, and so our staff was incredibly busy Sunday afternoon and Monday. I have been filling every spare minute calling my share."

Think of it: *Two hundred* personal calls to make—that is quite an effort, but Kevin and his staff *make* the time and create the opportunity to communicate with the parents. And Kevin does even more than that; I will relate that later in the chapter.

Early in my children's ministry journey, it never occurred to me to inform parents. When I learned more about being effective in ministry, I knew it was something I should do; but even then, I didn't imagine an even better response.

Responsibility #2: We Should Involve the Parents

There has been a huge improvement in awareness on the part of children's ministry leaders about the importance of parents in their children's journey. We all know that parent involvement is biblical and essential.

1. *Biblical*—We have memorized Deuteronomy 6:6-9 and Ephesians 6:4, and we are very familiar with other passages that instruct us that parents are primarily responsible for the spiritual training and nurture of their children. And we—all together—bemoan the fact that we are still struggling to get parents to do it.
2. *Essential*—If we want the best results. We know parents have far more influence on their children than we do, so we urge them to get involved.

I'm giving away my age by telling you this, but when our first child, Andrea, was born, hospitals didn't allow dads in the delivery room—at least our hospital didn't. I could be with Diane during labor, but when she was wheeled into delivery, I had to go out in the waiting room. By the time Ryan, our second, was born, the hospital had seen the light and changed their policy—they decided it was a *good* thing to let the dad come into the room, and so I got to be there.

Are we 30 years behind when it comes to the spiritual birth of a child? Are we like hospitals used to be? "Leave the birth up to the professionals" is the attitude that our practices reveal. I think that's a pretty smart idea with physical births, but I wonder if it is with spiritual births. When a child responds to the gospel, we are so eager to seal the deal that we don't seek parent participation. If we tell them, it's usually after the fact: "Johnny accepted Jesus today," we tell mom as she hurriedly picks up her boy after class. And that's the end of the involvement.

Kevin Harper does better than just inform; he involves. Kevin says, "It's our practice to ask the child to wait to make his or her decision until we can have both the child and the parent present—so we make an appointment, either at church or at their home. But we do that so that if at all possible, it is Mom or Dad who leads their child to Christ. We are there so that if they don't feel comfortable or if they aren't ready for some reason, we can either assist or lead them in that."

I applaud Kevin for what he has established. He says the additional effort that it takes to contact parents, make an appointment, and then work together with them concerning their child's decision is well worth it.

So, what if we don't involve parents? In particular, think of the consequences of *not* involving Christian parents:

- The parents may feel cheated. I felt cheated by not being in the room for Andrea's birth; Christian parents may very well feel the same way when their child experiences spiritual birth.
- The lack of parental involvement in their children's spiritual formation is only underscored. We bemoan the large number of Christian parents who leave spiritual instruction up to us; don't we only perpetuate that dependency when we are the only ones involved in their child coming to Christ?
- We miss an opportunity to draw parents into their child's spiritual growth. When a child trusts Christ, it is a choice opening for us to say, "Okay, now, parent, you need to help your child grow." And we can use the birth analogy to encourage them face to face to get involved like they maybe haven't been before.

In addition, we may miss an opportunity to share the gospel with unbelieving parents. If a child from a non-Christian family desires to accept Christ, it creates a natural opportunity to say to the parent, "Do you understand what it is your child desires to do?" What better opening is there to get to present the gospel to them?

Responsibility #3: We Should Instruct the Parents

Where do we expect children to come to Christ? Most of us, if we are honest, have event-centered or program-centered expectations; in other words, we plan VBS for the purpose of evangelizing kids; or special outreach events, or—as it was for me growing up—summer Bible camp. We ask, "How many children were saved at VBS this year?"

But we don't ask, "How many children were saved at home this year?" In our eagerness for numbers, I wonder—would we even count them?

Here's my premise: *The best place for a child who has a believing parent (or parents) to come to Christ is in the home.* Actually, that is my testimony; my mom and dad taught me about Jesus from the time I could understand, and when I was in my late 4s, I trusted Jesus as my Savior. For a long time, I felt deprived—because it was such a short, brief, undramatic testimony. I have come to realize, though, that it is the best kind.

Here's a second question: Who is the *best* person to lead a child to Christ? Whoever the *Holy Spirit* uses, of course! But maybe God uses the second-best, because the first-best isn't prepared to be involved in that decision. So let me ask it again: "Who is the *best* person to lead a child to Christ?" Wouldn't the answer, "The child's parent!" make a lot of sense?

Think of the benefits of encouraging parents to lead their own children to Christ:

- They would have a greater motivation to learn how to clearly present the gospel.
- The person with the most influence on the child (the parent) would feel more responsible for the growth of the child.

But will it count?

If you come from a church background where the practice of coming to Christ involves an action, then home-centered conversion experiences seem insufficient. Even when a child (or an adult, for that matter) trusts Christ somewhere other than church, we still want to see him or her walk down the aisle, stand up or meet with a counselor, or . . . you know what I mean. I've even heard this: "You need to publicly declare your faith—so if you trusted Christ at home, or by yourself, you need to come forward at church." While a public declaration of faith is an essential thing, my suspicion is that the motivation behind such urging is sometimes so that the preacher can count the new believer in his statistics.

We *are* a statistics-driven culture, aren't we? It has invaded our churches too. Many children's ministry leaders are under pressure from their senior pastor for results, and one of the most important is the number of children professing Christ as their Savior. Of course, we want to see results too—but we are not sure they should count unless they are underneath our control or at our event. We want to say, "We had *X* kids saved in VBS this year." If the number is great, we get more resources. If the number is small, we evaluate whether we should do it again. So what *if* a child accepts Christ at home? Does a children's ministry get to count it? Or are parents taking our job away from us—or at least our stats?

Maybe that shouldn't be the determining factor; instead, we ought to align our practices with what the Bible says.

What Does Scripture Say?

Households Came to Christ Together

While we all agree that salvation is an individual decision, Scripture recognizes the role of family (especially parents) in bringing someone to Christ.

I can't tell you the number of times I have quoted Acts 16:31 like this: "Believe on the Lord Jesus Christ, and you will be saved." I conveniently left off the last part of the sentence ("you and your household") because it didn't apply to the situation. Maybe I was talking to kids, or to an individual. But in looking back at my earlier years of ministry, I confess I left it off because I was uncomfortable with what it said—because it confused the issue that salvation is an individual decision. Evidently, Paul, in making this statement to the Philippian jailor, expected that when he trusted Christ, his whole household would as well.

I treated the passage as an isolated instance and, therefore, I ignored it. But then I began to notice other Scriptures that said similar things.

There was the story of the nobleman from Capernaum:
Then the father realized that this was the exact time at which Jesus had said to him, "Your son will live." So he and his whole household believed (John 4:53).

The story of the Roman centurion Cornelius:
He told us how he had seen an angel appear in his house and say, "Send to Joppa for Simon who is called Peter. He will bring you a message through which you and all your household will be saved" (Acts 11:13-14).

The story of Lydia:
One of those listening was a woman from the city of Thyatira named Lydia, a dealer in purple cloth. She was a worshiper of God. The Lord opened her heart to respond to Paul's message. When she and the members of her household were baptized, she invited us to her home (Acts 16:14-15).

The story of the Philippian jailor:
They replied, "Believe in the Lord Jesus, and you will be saved—you and your household" (Acts 16:31).

The account of Stephanas:
Yes, I also baptized the household of Stephanas; beyond that, I don't remember if I baptized anyone else (1 Cor. 1:16).

In each case, it is an adult coming to Christ; and the expectation (or the reality) was that the members of the household would follow—which likely included children. While these verses are not the best scriptural basis for involving parents when their children want to trust Christ, noting them does underscore the significance of family relationships in drawing people to Christ.

Why is a household saved together such a powerful thing? Picture an abandoned baby—one of the most inexplicable crimes. Now, consider when a child comes to Christ; if he or she is not welcomed into a "family" and nurtured, isn't the situation similar? I believe so.

Nurturing is significantly better if the parents do it. That thought links us to the second point.

Parents Are Responsible

I've noticed something. In all the chatter—and the passion—and the conversation about parents being involved in their children's spiritual growth, the issue is nearly always spiritual growth, but not so often about conversion. It is a rare occurrence when I hear parents being urged to present the gospel to their children and take responsibility for their understanding of how to become a Christian.

Yet, parents *are* responsible!

My friend Damon DeLillo[1] says that adults come to Christ through brokenness; children come to Christ through relationships. If that is true, generally speaking, why wouldn't we expect that God might use the closest relationships to draw a child to Himself?

Jesus said in John 6:44, "No one can come to me unless the Father who sent me draws them." When we say, "___ led someone to Christ," we really mean, "God used ___ to draw someone to Himself." Of course it is always God who does the saving, but He also chooses to use people as His instruments. And for children, those instruments of His choosing, in terms of principle, are parents, first of all. If parents are to bring their children up in the nurture and admonition of the Lord, as Ephesians 6:4 commands, would that include sharing the gospel with them and participating in their journey toward salvation, not merely discipling them afterward? A hundred times, yes! Of course it would.

Yet, parents feel ill equipped. Explaining the gospel on a child's level seems daunting to some; to others, they think the children's ministry leaders in the church are better equipped to share it. (That may be true for many; but isn't that a reason to train them?) Still others just expect that at church is where people get saved, which is a problem mindset that goes way beyond children's ministry.

So how will we get parents to get involved in their child's conversion? It will take, of course, communication, expectation and training.

Teaching Parents About Their Responsibility

My children's ministry friends, as a group, are generally discouraged about getting parents involved with their children's spiritual training. We have emphasized parent involvement for a number of years, but the successes are still infrequent. What is the first step of concern? How you are going to get parents to come to participate in training about leading their child to Christ. Few of them show up for meetings that are scheduled anyway.

I believe the key is in *when* you schedule them, so I recommend the following steps.

Schedule Parent Orientation

If you don't have a parent orientation as part of your ministry structure, you need to. I recommend two types: orientation for new parents and new department orientation. Think about when parents are most open to participating;

I have found there are two times. The first is when they make the decision to have their children attend regularly; the second is when there is a promotion to an older class. If you schedule promotions in the fall, as most churches do, that means you will want to have a department orientation scheduled soon after.

New Parent Orientation

Send home with a visiting child a brochure that welcomes both the child and the parents to your ministry. Tell the parents their child is welcome as a visitor, but when the family makes the decision to make it their regular church home, they must attend a parent orientation. If you don't find a way to create face-to-face communication with them, you will fail at getting their cooperation. If you call the homes of visiting children, make it part of your phone conversation to tell them that they will want to attend the orientation, and invite them to it.

Hold their little feet to the fire. Tell them later that you expect them to attend. Watch your attendance records, and when the visitors are coming regularly, remind them that they must come to the parent orientation. Tell them, "We want your child to have a wonderful experience here at church, and when you understand how we can partner together, we have the best opportunity to make that happen." And of course, get your senior pastor to tell parents they are required to attend.

With new parents, you'll need to be flexible in your scheduling—in fact, you must be prepared to do it one on one with individual parents if that is what timing requires. But you will certainly want to offer orientation regularly enough so that all parents get informed without going too many weeks into their child's involvement.

New Department Orientation

Most churches have an official time of the year when children are promoted to an older department. My observation is that this "promotion" usually consists of giving the children a gift and ushering them into a new room. Some churches do better; they prepare the children by letting them see the room ahead of time, and they give them an opportunity to meet their new teachers or even let them go in and participate before they are actually promoted.

Whenever children enter a new department, it is a time of angst for them, and probably for their parents as well. If you talk excitedly about the new department to the kids and let them experience it before they are actually a part of it, you will do a lot to help them feel at ease. In other words, an orientation plan for them is a good thing. But kids aren't the only ones who need a new orientation; parents need orienting as well. You will want them to meet their child's new teachers and understand new approaches and directions.

It also is a perfect time to encourage them to take the next step in doing what they can to lead their child to Christ.

You'll want to do the same as with new parent orientation; invite, invite, invite—then expect attendance, and follow up until all have gone through it.

In either type of orientation, you'll want to be strategic in what you communicate to parents. I recommend aligning your training with the ages of their child.

At birth (or baby dedication), set the vision for parents—that they will anticipate being part of their child's spiritual birth.

You might say these things: "Just as you have understood the significance of your child's birth, there is a second birth that is just as significant—his or her spiritual birth. You will want to be there for that, as well. That means that you must not leave it solely to children's workers here at church, but you must teach your child about Jesus and help your child understand what Jesus did for them on the cross."

In early childhood, explain to the parents the cautions (more about that to come), and talk about preparing their child's heart.

When children are promoted into the preschool class(es), parents need a new orientation or training. Parents need to be made aware that very young children—three-year-olds and four-year-olds—can respond to an urging to be saved just because the people who love them are encouraging them to do so, and not because they understand the gospel or because the Holy Spirit is drawing them. But very young children also *can* respond by faith as well—that is why it is critical that parents exercise discernment in guiding their child's faith response.

How do you prepare a preschooler's heart? Teach them about God—on their level: talk about how powerful He is, how He knows everything and how He sees everything. Teach them that God is holy, and even the smallest sin makes Him sad. Talk about how perfect heaven is. Help them learn what forgiveness is.

Remember that in biblical imagery, the heart is where a person *thinks*. So parents will want to help their preschoolers *think* about God. They will want to help mold the God-image in their child's worldview.

In early elementary, train parents how to explain the gospel and when to encourage their child to respond.

Most children trust Christ between the ages of 5 and 12, so when children enter this age group their parents need to be prepared to share the gospel with them. A parent orientation for early elementary will say to parents, "Your child is now entering the age window where he or she is most likely to respond to the gospel message." Begin by asking them, "Who would you like to lead your child to Christ?" If they say, "I would," then you ask them, "Are you clear about what to say?" and you have an opportunity to train them. If they respond, "Their children's ministry teacher," then you can ask them, "Well, wouldn't you like to be involved too?"

There's plenty in this book if you need content for training on presenting the gospel. Just consult the other chapters; they are a great resource!

But *when* do they encourage their child to respond? That's another topic to train parents on. I'll write more on that later, but my friend Kris Smoll[2] says she compares that decision to the choice about when to pull a loose tooth: as a parent, you often wonder if you should pull it, take your child to a professional so they can pull it or let it dangle for a few more days so that it can naturally fall out.

In middle school, train parents how to help their children validate their faith.

In their eagerness to want their kids to be confident in their salvation, parents can err in how they validate faith. An orientation for the parents of kids entering middle school would focus on how to confirm salvation.

Children at this age are entering into a life stage where they struggle more with the validation of their faith than at any other age. They're going through so many huge changes that they will naturally wonder how their faith fits in.

The Bible stories they learned in earlier years may not seem so relevant to the new relationships, new horizons and new independence that come with the tween years.

Parents need to *encourage* children to question whether their faith is real. If they don't, their kids will do it on their own, and it's better if they do it with Mom or Dad, rather than secretly, apart from them. "Is God real?" and "Am I really a Christian?" are healthy questions, not ones to be suppressed.

Help moms and dads ask faith questions of their children to discern their thinking. More than in the earlier years, parents need to be conversationalists in spiritual things. It is good at any stage; it is critical in the tween years. We can train parents to do it, and such training is critical at this stage of parenting.

Cautions for Parents

No matter the parenting stage, there are certain things alert parents will avoid. As we encourage parents to participate with their child's faith decision, there are issues that we want to help them avoid.

Watch for a Wrong Motivation.

Salvation comes as a result of faith, according to Romans 1:16, *NKJV*: "For I am not ashamed of the gospel of Christ, for it is the power of God to salvation for everyone who *believes*" (emphasis added). The belief referred to here is not mere head belief, but deep trust (the better meaning of the Greek word); so parents will want to discern if that is what is going on with their child.

In children's ministry, we need to watch for it too. I once observed a leader of a small group sharing the gospel with a nine-year-old girl. Later, the group leader announced, "Janni [I don't actually remember the girl's real name] came today for the very first time, and today she also accepted Jesus as her Savior!" I remember thinking, *I hope so.* But I wondered, *Was her response really one of faith? Nine-year-old girls usually love to please, and what if she responded to what the leader asked just because the lady was nice?* What would a nine-year-old do in an unfamiliar situation? And what if her response was not of faith, but was to simply please? Then, I think, she was not saved at that time—*but she was told she was.*

Parents are in a better position than a volunteer to discern what is going on in their child's heart. And if they sense that there is an additional motivation, then it is time to explain further, and encourage the child to wait until there is clearer understanding.

Here, in my opinion, are the big three "wrong motivations" for kids:

- *First, because they want to please someone.* Wrong motivations *can* be used to propel a child toward faith, and certainly God uses this one—a relationship—to draw children to Himself. But it can't be the reason why someone responds. Here's how it happened in my family.

  > Andrea was six, and excited about being a Christian. One after-noon, she and Ryan, who had just turned three, were playing in her bedroom. We had no idea of their topic of discussion when Andrea came running out into the kitchen with Ryan in tow and announced, "Ryan's now a Christian." Evidently, she had told him he needed to accept Jesus to become a Christian, and asked him, "Do you want to accept Jesus right now?" Three-year-old Ryan wanted to please his big sister, and he said yes. We knew, though, that he didn't have a clue what he was doing. We complimented Andrea on being so concerned about her brother, but we also made sure we continued to teach Ryan about the message of the gospel so that when the Holy Spirit drew him, he could make a genuine response.

- *Second, because they saw their friend (or brother or sister) get baptized.* After all, it looks pretty attractive. When you're baptized, you get to go in a pool of water, and everyone claps for you. Parents need to make sure there is not a motivation like this.
- *Third, because they want the grape juice.* We told our kids, who some-times were with us during Communion, that they had to be saved before they could partake of it. I can still remember the "this is un-fair" looks I got when we passed the elements right in front of them and they couldn't have any. I think it was made worse because it was usually about 11:45 AM, and they were hungry! Can you identify?

Avoid False Assurances

I shared this story in my first book *Rock Solid Kids:*[3]

At times I have had the privilege of interviewing missionary candidates. One candidate wife, Susan (not her real name), told this story about her "salvation" as a child.

"I grew up in a strong Christian family. We attended church regularly, and every summer, we kids would attend the Vacation Bible School at our church. I was scared of one of the teachers who was a very large, loud lady. My parents later told me she would brag to others in the church, 'No child ever comes through my VBS class without receiving Christ as Savior.'

"The year came when it was my turn to be in her class. I was petrified because my older siblings told me about her and what to expect. I didn't want to go, but my parents made me anyway. The loud lady's witnessing technique was to spend some time with each child away from the rest of the class, explain the way of salvation and ask them to respond. The day came when it was my turn. I went with her, but I wanted my 'turn' over as quickly as possible. 'Susan, do you know you're a sinner?' 'Yes.' 'Do you want to accept Jesus as your Savior?' 'Yes.' I was as agreeable as possible in order to get out of there fast. After she had me repeat a prayer, she had me write in my Bible, 'Today I became a Christian,' and then sign my name.

"I knew I hadn't really become a Christian, but for a number of years, when I would voice my doubts, my parents or people at my church would remind me, 'Don't you remember—you wrote it in your Bible?'

"I finally trusted in Christ when I was 16."

Susan's parents were trying to assure her that she was a Christian because of what she wrote in her Bible. Because they want their child to not have doubts, they will remind of some physical action to bolster confidence: "Don't you remember, you prayed with your Sunday School teacher when you were five?"

Our confidence of our relationship with God needs to find its foundation in two things: (1) Jesus paid the penalty for my sins on the cross, and (2) I trusted in what He did for the forgiveness of my sins.

Avoid Extreme Positions

Parents—even Christian ones—can have wildly opposite positions on the issue of their child trusting in Christ. Here are the two extremes:

- First, "I want my child to make his or her own decision." Some parents want a completely hands-off approach. Many non-Christian parents do, because they may see various religions as equal, or they may see spiritual things as not so important. But Christian parents also say this—and maybe some because they are so influenced by our culture of individualism. *Do* we want our children to make their own faith decisions? Of *course* we do, because in its essence, that is the only way one can become a Christian. None of us is a Christian because our parents were; we all must trust in Christ for ourselves. Knowing this, parents often make the statement above—but it can also mean, "I don't want to go to the trouble of teaching my child about Jesus" when doing that very thing is clearly commanded in Scripture.
- Second, pushing a child to make the decision. This is the opposite end of the spectrum: Parents who are so anxious for their child to be saved that they get ahead of the Holy Spirit and push them into a decision. I get a little squirmy when I hear a mom proclaim, "I've got four kids, and all of them accepted Jesus when they were four." I believe that can happen, but I don't see it as likely. I think it is more likely that the mom pushed her children into faith before they understood what was happening.

Parents, you must be in the middle. Be aware that your child's faith decision is all his or her own, or else it isn't genuine. You will want to communicate this to your kids: "You alone can make the decision to trust in Christ. I can't make it for you." Don't push—but at the same time, do all you can to teach and help them understand the gospel message. Listen and watch for signs that they are being drawn to God. Encourage sincere questions. And pray a *lot!*

If you are a children's worker, be sure to inform, include and instruct parents in the awesome, privileged role of leading a child to Christ. It is especially awesome when the child is their own. You don't want to miss it with yours; make sure you are creating the same privilege for others.

DISCUSSION QUESTIONS

1. Think back to the last time you had a child come to Christ in your ministry. How was a parent involved in that process?
2. In your ministry, who notifies the parents when a child trusts Christ?
3. What do you think of Larry Fowler's proposal that we clarify our intention up front with unbelieving parents to encourage children to make spiritual decisions?
4. Read Ephesians 6:4 again. How does it relate to parents being involved in their child's salvation experience?
5. Larry relates three consequences of *not* involving Christian parents. Which do you identify with the most, and why?
6. Think about the passages that mention whole households being saved (see John 4:53; Acts 11:13-14; 16:14-15; 16:31; 1 Cor. 1:16-17). What is your take on these passages?
7. How do you orient new parents to your children's ministry? Is it something you need to implement, or is it something already happening that could provide an opportunity for parents to be trained in leading their children to Christ?
8. In your children's ministry, is the "promotion" time targeted entirely at the child? What do you think of using it as an opportunity to orient parents anew?
9. Fowler recommends four levels of training for parents (at birth, early childhood, early elementary and middle school). Are any of these present in your ministry now? Which could you begin to implement?
10. Which of the "Cautions for Parents" have you personally observed? What are your feelings about making sure parents are aware of these?

Notes

1. Damon is Family Ministries Director at Mission Church in Ventura, California, and the Creative Director at Gospel Light.
2. Kris Smoll is the Director of Children's Ministry at Appleton Alliance Church in Appleton, Wisconsin.
3. Larry Fowler, *Rock Solid Kids* (Ventura, CA: Gospel Light, 2004), pp. 120-121.

PART 4:

What Do You Want the Outcomes to Be?

13

Discipleship Cookbook: What a Discipled Kid Looks Like

ROGER FIELDS

At the age of five, in a Bullwinkle costume, I learned that life would have lots of twists and turns. I was lost and trying to find my way home on a dark Halloween night. Unsure of where I was going, and struggling to see through a Bullwinkle mask with my, as yet, undiagnosed poor vision, my most vivid childhood memory was made. I didn't realize then that much of life involves trying to figure out how to get someplace without looking silly.

Today, I am a city slicker living on a horse farm, trying to keep the place mowed while not stepping in something. With my hottie horsewoman wife, four daughters, six horses, chocolate lab and cat named Bob, life is never dull.

I like chocolate. I'm fashion challenged except that I recently discovered I like things from J.Crew. I rock at *Dr. Mario,* and I would eat at Qdoba every day of the week if I could. I'd like to be able to slam-dunk a basketball before I'm 65. With the exception of Pop Tarts, chocolate donuts, candy bars, pumpernickel bread, Jones sodas and ice cream, I try to eat right. I spend all of my time writing, traveling, doing farm chores, and creating computer graphics. When I'm not travelling . . . well, never mind, I'm pretty much always travelling.

And I started Kidz Blitz in 1996 (what a wild ride that has been). You can read all about it in my book *Jumping the Track.* Go to http://rogerfields.com/rogers-book-jumping-the-track/ for more info on the book that details my life, ministry and journey to Kidz Blitz.

Stuff I've Done . . . Really!

- Planted and pastored two churches (Kentucky and Florida)
- Written lots of articles (some I don't claim anymore)
- Graduated from an unknown Bible college
- Been to hundreds of churches across America conducting Kidz Blitz family events (seen it all)
- Taught countless (countless, not worthless) workshops
- Bungee jumped (and survived). Do it again? Hmmm, no.
- Served as a consultant to churches
- Studied computer science at the University of Kentucky (did not like anything about that)
- Repaired cable TV towers 600 feet straight up (looked down on a helicopter!!!). What was I thinking?
- Had four (as in FOUR . . . 4!) daughters
- Celebrated our 30-year anniversary
- Did stand-up comedy once (that was enough)
- Spoke at conferences

Ministry is about leaving people better than you found them. It is about outcome. It is about producing something. It is about making something profound.

"Go therefore and *make disciples* of all the nations, baptizing them in the name of the Father and of the Son and of the Holy Spirit" (Matt. 28:19, *NKJV*).

Our job is not merely to spout information, entertain, educate or even inspire. It is to craft something, to shape something, to build something: disciples.

Jesus sent us out to make: not attenders, not department workers, not good citizens, not even ministers, but much more. Jesus told us to go and make disciples.

So what—pray tell—is a disciple? Really? What is it? How can you make something if you are not clear on what it is you are making?

My first real job as a teenager was working for a civil engineering firm in Lexington, Kentucky. I was hired to make core boxes. They told me I would have a shop, power tools and all the lumber I wanted. All I had to do was ride my bicycle to work and make enough core boxes to keep them supplied. I was thrilled to get my first non-paper-route job.

There was only one small problem: I had no idea what a core box looked like. What's a core box? I knew I could measure wood, saw boards in two, hammer stuff together and use a screwdriver. But without a clear picture of what a core box was supposed to be, I was clueless about how to proceed. How long should I cut the wood? How big do they want the box? What shape should it be? Where should I nail it together? Should I use screws? Should a core box look like a shoebox or a music box? I had lots of questions. I needed to see a core box. Once I understood the expected outcome, it was easy to move forward. I knew what to do—once I had a clear picture of what I was supposed to make.

What Is a Disciple?

What is your picture of a disciple? What does one look like? What is a disciple supposed to be? How can you spot one? What are the characteristics? It's difficult to build anything when you don't know what the finished product should look like.

We tend to define a disciple based solely on externals. Does Harriet serve in the church? Does George still cuss? Is Thelma gossiping about the pastor's wife? Is Henry looking for a job? While God's grace certainly does impact our actions, it cannot be the sole indicator that one is a disciple. One can, for instance, serve in the church, stop gossiping, refrain from cussing, hold down a job and have no authentic relationship with Jesus. Would that person be the kind of disciple Jesus wants us to produce? Surely there is a higher purpose than merely cranking out good citizens who serve in a church department.

Then what is it? I ask again. What really is a disciple? If we can't define them, how can we make them?

The big secret is this: Being a disciple is more thrilling than what we might have thought. It's not about education or grueling service or sacrifice. It's about so much more. The word itself, "disciple," does not sound particularly gripping. But the ideas behind it are amazing.

It is not about conducting trendy worship experiences, transferring spiritual information or even modifying behavior. It goes beyond all of this.

While the definition of a disciple is not as clear-cut as a core box, Jesus gave us specific characteristics that can guide us. No place in the Bible defines what it means to be a disciple better than John 15:7-8.

Here's the recipe:

If you abide in Me, and My words abide in you, you will ask what you desire, and it shall be done for you. By this My Father is glorified, that you bear much fruit; so you will be *my disciples* (John 15:7-8, *NKJV*, emphasis added).

Let's peel this apart—carefully.

Live in Jesus

A disciple "abides" in Jesus. The word means to live.

He lives in Jesus. He doesn't merely know facts about Jesus. He goes beyond information. For a disciple, Jesus is more than an example. Jesus is someone to "abide" in. He experiences the life of Jesus from within.

He knows Jesus beyond the flesh. In other words, a disciple knows Jesus beyond the Man in the Gospels who walked in sandals 2,000 years ago. He knows Jesus today.

"Even though we have known Christ according to the *flesh*, yet now we know Him thus *no longer*" (2 Cor. 5:16, *NKJV*, emphasis added).

He no longer knows Jesus merely as the bearded traveler in Matthew, Mark, Luke and John. He knows more than the historical Jesus. He used to know Him only from what he read in the Gospels. But he now moves beyond head knowledge into personal relationship. He knows Him today. He knows the Jesus who is alive and well and active today. A disciple abides in Him.

He doesn't base his relationship with Jesus on his own performance. He knows it's not about what he did for God; it's about what God did for him. It's not about picking the correct fruit from the Tree of Knowledge of Good and Evil; it's about partaking from the Tree of Life—Jesus. Behavior modification is not the objective. Being fully alive in Jesus is the objective.

Paul, the apostle, said it best: "I have been crucified with Christ; it is *no longer I who live*, but Christ lives in me; and the life which I now live in the flesh I live by faith in the Son of God, who loved me and gave Himself for me" (Gal. 2:20, *NKJV,* emphasis added).

Paul's words are a game changer. To get the full impact, think of what he did not say. "I'm doing my best living for Jesus." "I'm striving to be the best I can be." "I'm serving the Lord every day." That is the language we use.

Instead, Paul reveals the secret: He is crucified, and Jesus lives through him. Paul sees the cross as an exchange. He exchanged his life for the life of Jesus. Paul knew what it meant to abide in Jesus.

He considered himself dead, thus allowing the life of Jesus to move through him. When the life of Jesus flows through you, there is much less striving. Less frustration. Less discouragement.

Paul also describes this exchanged life as a mystery. "To them God willed to make known what are the riches of the glory of this *mystery* among the Gentiles: which is *Christ in you,* the hope of glory" (see Col. 1:27).

By "mystery," Paul means "Christ in you" is something surprising that does not make much sense to our human brain. It is a truth that is hard to comprehend but can be experienced.

I want kids to begin their life's journey with Jesus—not striving to serve Him—but by experiencing Jesus as He lives through them.

Words Abide Inside

"My words abide in you" means that Jesus' words are alive in a disciple. Not just what He said, but what He says. Disciples listen to what Jesus is saying to them now. This is not merely about learning Bible verses, but also about listening to the Lord daily.

The writer of Hebrews quotes the book of Psalms to make the point that unless our hearts become hard, we can listen to the Lord every day. Jesus has something to say to you every day. If your heart is not hard, you will hear Him. "Today, if you hear His voice, do not harden your hearts" (Heb. 4:7; Ps. 95:7-8, *NKJV*).

Memorizing is good; listening is better. Nothing you hear from God will contradict what He has said in the Bible, but reading is not enough to sustain a vibrant walk with Jesus. You have to be able to hear Him speak in your heart. Disciples do that. They listen.

I want kids to grow in their ability to hear the voice of Jesus in their heart.

"Desire" Is Not a Dirty Word

"Ask what you desire" follows the admonition to abide in Jesus and listen to Him. First abide. Next listen. Then, one's desires change. A disciple's desires change to align with what God desires. He or she begins to want the same stuff that God wants.

We tend to think of all desires as something to be avoided. When the Christian community uses the word, it normally means sex, drugs, theft, and so on. We seldom use the word in a positive sense. Buddhism teaches that all desire is wrong. The Bible does not.

Desires are not necessarily based on selfishness. And we should not assume that every desire from God will be a drudgery. We tend to think that if something we want will be enjoyable, then it must not be from God. God is good. He is not trying to beat your life into some sort of miserable existence.

There is a lot of space between a selfish desire and a gloomy sacrifice. Sometimes we want something that is purely self-serving. Sometimes we assume that God wants something so sacrificial that it will strip all the fun out of living. Jesus will show you the space in the middle.

Since "desire" has a negative connotation within much of the Christian community, take a look at these verses of Scripture (emphasis added):

May He grant you according to your heart's *desire*, And fulfill all your purpose (Ps. 20:4, *NKJV*).

You have given him his heart's *desire*, And have not withheld the request of his lips (Ps. 21:2, *NKJV*).

Delight yourself also in the LORD, And He shall give you the *desires* of your heart (Ps. 37:4, *NKJV*).

The fear of the wicked will come upon him, And the *desire* of the righteous will be granted (Prov. 10:24, *NKJV*).

Hope deferred makes the heart sick, But when the *desire* comes, it is a tree of life (Prov. 13:12, *NKJV*).

Apparently, desires can be good.

A discussion emerged in my men's group about following God's leading. The examples they gave were about living in poverty, moving to some remote location, giving up their job, or some other difficult challenge. "Is God in the misery business?" I asked. "Does He ever want anything enjoyable for us?" That never dawned on them. They never thought about God asking them to do something they actually had a desire to do.

God led the people out of Egypt and eventually into the land of milk and honey, not the land of rocks and snakes. God had something good in store, something they could desire.

A disciple grows in his desires. He prays for what he desires. God answers. They see what they "ask" for in their prayers answered.

Since God is a good Father who enjoys blessing His children, we can expect Him to want the best for us (emphasis added):

If you then, being evil, know how to *give good gifts* to your children, how much more will your Father who is in heaven give good things to those who ask Him! (Matt. 7:11, *NKJV*).

Every *good gift* and every *perfect gift* is from above, and comes down from the Father of lights, with whom there is no variation or shadow of turning (Jas. 1:17, *NKJV*).

Flash! God may want you to do something you might actually enjoy. I want kids to begin wanting what God wants.

Just Ask

"Ask what you desire" means just that. Ask. Prayer is not a spiritual disci-pline. It is talking to our Father God who hears and answers. Prayer produces an outcome. Ask 100 Christians to name a characteristic of a disciple and chances are good that no one will include answered prayer. But Jesus did.

I hope my kids don't consider talking to me as a discipline, something that requires effort. I would like to think they enjoy talking to me. I certain-ly enjoy hearing from them and talking to them. And I particularly enjoy meeting their requests when I can. Am I a better dad than our heavenly Father? I think not.

Reducing prayer to a discipline diminishes the relationship we have to our Father. "For you did not receive the spirit of bondage again to fear, but you received the Spirit of adoption by whom we cry out, 'Abba, Father'" (Rom. 8:15, *NKJV*). "Abba" is the Aramaic equivalent of "daddy." That doesn't sound like a discipline to me. That sounds like a toddler talking to his or her father.

We have turned prayer into an exercise and fabricated excuses as to why God doesn't answer. But He does answer if you can avoid two ditches. James sums it up:

> You lust and do not have. You murder and covet and cannot obtain. You fight and war. Yet you do not have because you do not ask. You ask and do not receive, because you ask amiss, that you may spend it on your pleasures (Jas. 4:2-3, *NKJV*).

1. Don't Be Afraid to Ask

Most Christians never ask for anything significant. What would you think if your own kids never asked for anything—ever? You would conclude that they didn't believe you could, or would, grant their request. Somehow, we have the notion that God resents us asking Him for anything.

"But, Roger," the objections rise, "God is not interested in blessing us with stuff." He is not interested in us building our lives around material goods, but in the Bible, God actively provided for people. And here's the shocker: He provided for people *beyond* their bare necessities.

"But, Roger," the objections mount, "God provides our needs, not our greeds." I agree, but there is a lot of space between needs and greeds. I don't need a car. I could walk, take the bus or bum rides from my friends. But is it greedy for me to want my own transportation? I don't think so.

God gave Adam the Garden of Eden. According to the description, it was about 1,500 square miles. Did Adam *need* a garden the size of Texas? I don't think so.

We often put too much importance on material goods. We live in a world made of tangible stuff. But the Bible is filled with God responding to material requests, and not all of them are "needs." Nobody "needed" more wine at the wedding feast where Jesus performed His first miracle. I would have thought Jesus would have done something more significant for His first miracle.

Read what Malachi said to the cranky people of his day:

"Your words have been *harsh* against Me," says the LORD, "yet you say, 'What have we spoken against You?' You have said, 'It is useless to serve God; what *profit* is it that we have kept His ordinance, and that we have walked as mourners before the LORD of hosts?'" (Mal. 3:13-14, *NKJV*, emphasis added).

The people in Malachi's day complained that there was no "profit" (material benefit) to serving God. The Lord says that was a harsh thing to say. When we claim that God is not interested in blessing people materially, we are saying something harsh against God. If one of my kids claimed that I never wanted to help her materially, that would be a harsh accusation. Be careful about being so spiritual that you think you are above needing God to help you financially of materially.

While we seek God's kingdom (His plans) first, other things get added to the mix. God designed it that way: "But seek first the kingdom of God and His righteousness, and all these things shall be *added* to you" (Matt. 6:33 *NKJV*, emphasis added).

That's the secret. Seek God and expect Him to add. Don't seek stuff and expect God to be thrown in as an extra.

2. Don't Ask for Anything that Hurts Others

Murder and covetousness hurt other people. To murder means you take a life. To covet means you want to take someone's stuff. That's what "asking amiss" is about. In this context, "lusting" is to want something that would in some way degrade someone else.

It's one thing to ask God to provide or to solve a problem. It is quite another to ask God for something simply because Harry next door owns something you want. We need to be able to make the distinction. Not all requests are created equally. There is a profound difference between a child of God asking his Father for provision and a child of God wanting to get ahead of, or even hurt, another child of God.

A disciple is not afraid to ask God for help, for a solution or for provision. He trusts his heavenly Father and is able to ask Him with childlike faith. He isn't self-absorbed, but neither is he timid. "So let us come *boldly* to the throne of our gracious God. There we will receive his mercy, and we will find grace to *help us* when we need it most" (Heb. 4:16, *NLT*, emphasis added).

I want kids to grow in healthy desires so they can ask their Father in heaven and see their prayers answered.

Making Jesus Look Cool

"By this My Father is glorified" means that the life of a disciple tends to make God look attractive.

Let's strip away sappy religious language and say it straight up. When people look at a disciple, they should give God the credit. They should realize how cool God is when they look at a disciple.

Disciples make Jesus famous.

"But sanctify the Lord God in your hearts, and always be ready to give a defense to everyone who *asks* you a reason for the hope that is in you, with meekness and fear" (1 Pet. 3:15, *NKJV*, emphasis added). You shouldn't have to beat people over the head to make them want Jesus. They should be asking questions about what energizes you.

I want kids to cause others to want Jesus.

Fruit Happens

"Bear much fruit" means that what is inside of you comes out naturally, the way a tree bears fruit. Relationship with Jesus was never meant to be a struggle. Most Christians look at the Christian life the way a spawning salmon looks at the rapids. They see a tough struggle upstream against the current.

Apple trees do not struggle to produce apples. The life in the tree naturally produces apples. That's what healthy apple trees do. They produce fruit.

The Holy Spirit is the same way. He does stuff in—and through—disciples. Surprising stuff. Refreshing stuff. Cool stuff. All without sweating over it. There is a reason the Bible calls it "fruit." It's because it's something the life inside of us produces and manifests on the outside. Inward life produces outward characteristics. "But the *fruit* of the Spirit is love, joy, peace, longsuffering, kindness, goodness, faithfulness, gentleness, self-control" (Gal. 5:22-23, *NKJV*, emphasis added).

Some Christians make it hard to be a Christian. Some Christian speakers, authors and pastors make living the Christian life under grace harder than living as a Jew under the Law. Think about that. Under the Law, the Jews had to sacrifice a few animals, celebrate some annual feasts, cut pork out of their diet and obey a few other simple rules. It wasn't all that tough when you think about it.

Living under grace is supposed to be easier than living under the Jewish Law. But to hear some Christians talk about it, you would think otherwise. They make you feel guilty if you don't read all the way through your Bible every year, pray three times a day, witness regularly, serve faithfully in the church for years with no end in sight, be a model parent/spouse, go on annual mission trips . . . the list goes on and on.

Consider this: If your version of Christianity is harder to live up to than it is to live up to the Jewish Law, your version is too tough. Your boot camp style is destined to frustrate and discourage believers of every sort.

Hence, all the various spiritual growth programs designed to "help" you live the Christian life. *Flash!* Jesus is the only one who actually lived the Christian life. Now He just wants you to get out of the way so that He can live it through you.

No program can replace the fruit-producing life of Jesus. No curriculum can "educate" a kid into being alive in Jesus. It is a supernatural outworking of the life of Jesus inside that cannot be reduced to a formula. There is no recipe. There are no steps. There are no principles. This is not a human work; it is a spiritual phenomenon.

I'm more energized about helping a kid allow Jesus to live through him than I am about modifying his behavior. I want to lead kids to the Tree of Life, not help them pick the right fruit from the Tree of Knowledge of Good and Evil.

I want kids to bear fruit without struggling.

Ideas

A discipled kid—or adult, for that matter—is not someone who merely makes effective choices; it is someone who allows the life of Jesus to flow through him or her. Discipleship is not a program. It is not a curriculum. It is not about educational material to be memorized. It is about the life of Jesus that flows from the inside to the outside.

Hold up Jesus to the kids in your children's ministry. Here are some ideas about ways to talk to the kids in your children's ministry:

1. Talk about how you relate to Jesus in everyday circumstances.
2. Tell about times when Jesus taught you something.
3. Talk about how Jesus encourages you.
4. Talk about times when Jesus did something through you that you could not have done by yourself.
5. Talk about times when a prayer was answered.

Big truths expand one's life; little rules constrict one's life. Growing into the big truth of being alive in Jesus has more impact than walking away from little no-nos. To be a disciple is to be fully alive—alive in Jesus.

DISCUSSION QUESTIONS

1. What comes to mind when you hear the word "disciple"?
2. Why do you think Jesus used a vine to illustrate discipleship?
3. What do you think of when you hear the word "desire"?
4. What do you think the difference is between knowing Bible information in your head and experiencing the life of Jesus living through you?
5. How would you describe the difference between wrong desires and good desires? What are examples?
6. How could Jesus living through you make Him attractive to others?

14

Equipping Children to Be Missional

BETH GUCKENBERGER

Beth and her husband, Todd, live with their family in Monterrey, Mexico, where they serve with Back2Back Ministries, an international orphan care ministry headquartered in Cincinnati, Ohio. They both graduated from Indiana University with degrees in education; and between biological, foster and adopted, they are raising nine children. Currently, the ministry has operations on three different continents (Mexico, India and Nigeria). The Guckenbergers have lived in Monterrey since 1997; and in that time, they have hosted thousands of guests on the ministry campus.

Beth is the author of *Reckless Faith* (Zondervan, 2008); *Relentless Hope* (Standard Publishing, 2010); *Tales of the Not Forgotten* (Standard Publishing, 2012); and *Tales of the Defended Ones* (Standard Publishing, 2013). Beth is the recipient of the 2013 International Network of Children's Ministry Legacy Award and the

Cincinnati Christian University's 2012 Salute to Leaders Award for her and Back2Back's impact on children internationally. She travels and speaks regularly at conferences, youth gatherings and church services. Beth is also a co-host on *Real Life, Real Talk* on Saturdays at 8:00 AM on Sirius-XM 131. Her topics include, but are not limited to, orphan care; missions; ministry; parenting; marriage/intimacy; and general faith. Her style is storytelling, and she draws from her field experience as a missionary and parent of nine children for illustrations of biblical concepts.

I was sitting inside an orphanage in Mazatlan, Mexico, this past week and listening to the directors of that home lament that their older kids are too focused on their own needs, and not aware enough of the suffering of others. We were brainstorming how they could take the work God was doing in their own lives and share it with others who need encouragement. We were fighting the notion that they needed to travel somewhere to do it, or that they needed training or a class. In reality, they didn't need anything other than a friendship with someone and some intentionality. When we look outside of ourselves, when we seek to meet the needs of others, when we share what God is doing in our hearts, we connect what has been broken. That's the simplest definition of missions I can think of.

I could have been having this conversation in a living room in the Midwest, or in any other country. We adults long for children to see how God wants to use them in a world lost.

I sat in on a call to a children's magazine with other contributing editors and we spent two hours thinking of ways—through articles and contests and blog posts—we could write to encourage adults to invite children into the Great Commission. We brainstormed and networked and fought the easy path of a program or a plan. We knew that God's way was relational and invitational, but our default button wanted steps to follow.

I had coffee with a friend whose 10-year-old daughter is curious about how her family's faith can be shared with others; her mother is afraid that if she shares openly about God, she will experience rejection. She asked for help in how to prepare her for this kind of evangelism, the kind that sticks around long after the hands go up (or don't).

Wherever we Christians are gathered, this topic of missional living eventually arises. And if we take seriously the raising of the next generation, then missional living for our children is close to our hearts. In reality, it shouldn't look like a mini-version or a toned-down version, or a watered-down version of ours, because Jesus was continually telling *us* to live as children, not children to live like us. To look honestly at how to teach children to share their faith is to look honestly at how we are doing ourselves.

If we believe this is true, that how God loves us and came to us should be in our conversations with others, believers and skeptics alike, how should it/ could it spill over into our relationships and priorities? When and how and where do we engage our children?

As a 16-year overseas missionary and a mother to nine, this is a subject I have deeply wrestled with. My opinions on children being missional have been all over the board. Sometimes I insisted that my children just wanted to be kids, not missionaries, and I filled them with fruit snacks and video games, making sure they didn't pay the price for my following a call. At other times, I thought they need to be mini-mes; I hauled them to squatters' villages and orphanages, and asked them to offer themselves and often extrinsically motivated them, rather than working to cultivate hearts that overflow with God's love for those who are needy.

In this messy world of parenting, I am learning a better rhythm—a rhythm of listening and responding, of relationships and conversations not easily wrapped up in a sound byte or a craft. I have decided that the process of working out my faith in front of my children (and that means the sacrifice, the unknown, the rejection) is important. With that in mind, here are some principles I am adopting in this missional, Great-Commission-living-and-parenting lifestyle.

Invite Children into the "Sufferings of Christ"

It is our instinctive nature to put a protective shield around our children. But to cultivate empathy, our children need to see how much love can cost us. Love cost Christ everything, and He invites us into that lifestyle, knowing that we cannot outgive Him. The more we pour out on His behalf, the more He will fill us up. The Greek word *agape* in the Bible has a great big long definition in the Greek, but my favorite phrase is "compelled to action." It was *agape* love that compelled Christ to the cross and *agape* love that children innocently give voice to when they offer their snack to a friend or want to sacrificially give a new toy away. We do them a disservice when we silence them or tell them that what they want to do/offer/give is not necessary.

I was speaking recently at a chapel in an orphanage in Mexico, and I told the kids about another orphanage in Haiti. The Haitian orphanage was struggling to provide protein in their meals and fresh vegetables; they were simply too costly. I asked the Mexican orphans to consider what we could do about it. What options did we have? How could we respond? These are kids who have no money. After some discussion, one nine-year-old boy, Emi, said that they had themselves to offer. He mentioned that he was strong (despite having an arm in a cast at the time). They all listened to him and agreed that they could offer themselves. By the end of the day, we had organized and executed a car wash, raising several hundred dollars to send to the orphanage in Haiti. It cost the kids that day a lot; it cost time and effort and a free Sunday afternoon; but they were so full by the day's end, no one noticed. That's God economy.

When we ask our children to give more than their leftovers to God (broken toys, outgrown clothes), we model for them Christ's teaching. In the book of Malachi, God warns about giving our blemished lambs and expecting them to pass as acceptable. The Israelites knew what their best was and held that back. God sent them a warning, and it's one we can still hear echoed today. We need to teach our children from the start that God wants our very best. We have the chance to invite them to pay a bit of the cost (sacrificing a birthday gift, giving up an afternoon), believing the short-term "pain" will reap in their character a long-term benefit.

I was talking to a group of moms the other day about the temptation to make our children the center of our kingdoms. To manipulate and educate and control and reward and then hope at the end of all our efforts that out pops a kid who is others-centered. It's not possible. When we live missionally, as a family, there are costs and benefits. It is natural to want them to experience all the benefits and minimize their costs, but that doesn't serve them in the end. To see the character I want developed in my children, I have to ask him or her to pick up heavy things; that's how those muscles get exercised.

Service Is a Three-Step Process: Look, Listen and Offer

We can teach our children to see what they have in their hands. (What are their resources? What are their gifts? Who are their relationships?) Then we teach them and model for them how to listen for whom God is putting on their heart. (A neighbor? A cousin? Someone from school? Someone they have never met?)

Then we simply bridge the two—what we have and who we have a heart for.

When I talk to children about missions, I explain my heart for orphans as a "burr under my saddle." I can't sit still or comfortably when I think about parentless children. It compels me to act. The first time I felt the burr was when I saw children who were hungry and hiding the food I brought to them under their mattresses. After that, I was never the same.

The children in your life might have burrs in their saddles for kids on their soccer team, or people they see in their school who are lonely or new or have special needs. Burrs can develop for people we know and for people we see on TV who are victims of violence or natural disaster. All burrs start with a cry, and God tunes us each into a cry that reflects the heart and story He is developing for each of us.

Once, I took all of my children horseback riding on some trails in the mountains. Trail rides are where horses go to retire. They all know how to go out to the destination and then return home. They don't need to be steered; it's second nature to them.

When the horse handler saw that I wasn't paying much attention to his class before the ride (because I was filling out a lot of release forms and had put on my form that I had some riding experience), I think he decided this city slicker needed to learn a lesson. He gave all of my children old horses (which I was glad for them), but for me, he brought out a 16-hand-high horse that literally looked like she was dancing.

I swung up on her back and we rode for a while; I felt like I was getting my money's worth for this adventure. My horse wasn't tired or old like the others; she was fun! However, after a while, this crazy horse wasn't settling down, and we were coming up to a difficult part in the path on the side of a mountain. I wanted her footing to be sure on the rocky path, so I humbled myself and shouted to the horse wrangler, "What do you think is going on with my horse?"

After watching us for a couple of moments, he said, "It looks like she must have a little burr in her saddle, but . . ." he looked down at his watch, "give her another minute or two; we've been out here long enough. I bet whatever is bothering her will rub itself numb and she should calm down in a minute."

Sure enough, that's exactly what happened. When we got to the part of the trail I was worried about, my horse had calmed down significantly, and whatever had been bothering her wasn't any longer. She spent the rest of the ride looking like the other horses, head bent down, following the rear in front of her. I spent the rest of the ride thinking to myself about what happens when we ignore the burrs under our saddles. They eventually rub to the point of a callous and then grow numb. As a result, on the rest of the trail ride of life, we don't get a much better view than the rear end of the horse in front of us.

But, we have a choice!

We can listen to the cry that represents the burr in our saddles and respond to it; it's our insurance policy against growing numb. When we hear our children raise questions, offer insights or sound unsatisfied with how someone is living, it's our chance to listen with them to the burr in their own saddles and walk with them as we help them know what their next steps can be.

I often ask children what makes them feel uncomfortable (a lonely child in their classroom, hungry people they know or see on TV, a neighbor's story) and then share how that is a piece of God's heart deposited in them. All they need to do is offer what they have (reminding them they have more than just objects: they have time, they have a smile, they have ideas, they have prayers) to those they see. Andy Stanley says, "Do for one what you wish you could do for all." Kids don't need to understand causes or evangelistic campaigns; they don't and won't see things at the macro level. They will, however, see stories and friends and names. Keeping their next steps personal will drive engagement and set them up for a lifestyle of reaching out to others in His name.

Teach Children About the Exchange

Service is not a one-way street. In the end, that kind of giving creates dependency with those we want to reach and gives children a false sense of accomplishment. We have so much more to offer than our money and goods. The gospel is about what has already been done, and we are the testifiers to His good news! Sharing about how the gospel is changing our lives and shaping our decisions means a conversation, a relationship. Does your lifestyle allow for time to have relationships? Are you talking as a family about what you can receive from those you are sharing your life with? As Paul said, "We were delighted to share with you not only the gospel of God, but our lives as well" (1 Thess. 2:8). The Great Commission is not something to be checked off a list; it's a lifestyle of inviting others into the stories God is writing for your family. It's pointing them not to you, not to liking you, but to Jesus.

One of the biggest barriers to adults serving is belief that they have anything to offer. We have a chance to model for our children—everyone has a listening ear, a smile, counsel, company, education, and the list goes on. Dropping off toys or sending in checks is one step, but that alone won't cultivate a missional heart in your child (or in you!).

What happens when we don't exchange with someone is that we develop an us and them attitude. We have so much; they have so little. We are so great, we know Jesus, and they are so lost, they don't. On the other side of that equation are still people. People who don't know better, who formed their own worldviews from their own experiences. We, as representatives of the gospel, would serve them well by listening more than talking, and exchanging with them more than handing off.

There is a tremendous movement in missions to not create dependency, and we have the torch to pass on to the next generation. They can learn from the mistakes we have made (even well-intentioned efforts can do more harm).

A large missions organization encouraged children to send in jars of peanut butter with two quarters taped to the lid to an address in Miami, Florida, following the earthquake in Haiti. Thousands of jars arrived to be shipped over, the quarters representing the cost of that jar's freight. The children felt good, the parents felt better, and all seemed well.

However, one of the only viable crops in Haiti is peanuts! When jars and jars of free peanut butter arrived in the port of Haiti, it harmed the local economy more than it helped the recipients. We can be smart about how we help these days; we have the chance to teach our children to be the same.

Model for them your own relationship with the lost world. Show them the world is bigger than your family. When we make all of our efforts, resources and time about the maintaining and growing up of our own world, we miss out on how God might want to enrich our life with missions storylines.

A friend of mine told me about how he was walking with his oldest son in their neighborhood and saw some trash along the sidewalk. He pointed it out to his son and asked him to pick it up, mentioning how we need to keep our neighborhood clean, and so on. It was a typical parenting opportunity and he felt good that he had seized it to share that message.

Later that month, he heard his middle son complaining to his mom that when he was in the neighborhood earlier with the big brother, riding bikes, his brother made him pick up some trash on the side of the road. The father realized that his oldest son heard the message that *we need to keep our neighborhood clean,* but he also heard inadvertently, *when you see trash, tell someone younger/weaker to take care of it.* It didn't matter what he, the father, had said; it mattered what the boy had witnessed. It was what he saw that he modeled. If the father had simply picked up the trash, maybe using words, or maybe not, a different message might have been absorbed.

We need to model for our children what missional living looks like. Just telling them to have a missional heart will not produce fruit. Doing crafts involving maps won't do it. It will take root when they witness your desire to share your faith. Then the message will be heard loud and clear.

Do they see you talk to the clerk in the store? Do they see you offer your help to a neighbor? Do they see you take time to reach out to those you work with? Process with them after they overhear a conversation; let them know what you were thinking, how you were hoping it might go, how you are excited about a response or discouraged and know more prayer is needed. Make those kinds of conversation a regular part of your family.

Start with the Teachable Moment, Not the Long Devotional

World issues and injustices can creep into our everyday conversations. While you are driving or at the dinner table, have a matter-of-fact discussion that, for example, a billion people on the planet don't have clean water. Make it concrete, and mix their water at dinner with a little ice tea powder so it looks dirty. Or send your kids marching around the house 10 times with a bucket on their head full of water. Share with them how far a child their age walks for water around the world. Make the conversation come alive.

Introduce them to people, places and the realities of a lost world. You be the dispenser of these facts, not the TV or school. They will learn the truth eventually. There *are* children who are slaves; there *are* natural disasters that destroy communities and families; there *is* war. It's always better to frame it than have to later react to it. Allow them opinions and questions. Take a moment to look up something online, or share a story you heard or a YouTube video. Between soccer practice and homework, they will repeat and remember these conversations of substance. It's always worth the time it takes.

To have these teachable moments, however, we have to be plugged in to each other, not to other electronic devices. It means that we have to be comfortable wandering into conversations without having all the answers; to be vulnerable with our kids that maybe we don't know why hard things happen, or why someone doesn't want to hear about the gospel. We can share our disappointments: "I had hoped that would go differently."

By sharing the hard moments of missional living, as well as the good ones, we demonstrate that the results are not ours to control. One of the most common complaints I hear from my work with teenagers is that they don't see adult Christians sharing their disappointments; so when something doesn't go well for the teens, they assume they have done it wrong. We have the opportunity to model for them that our job is to listen, to be open, to share, to offer, and then allow the Lord to do the rest. We can allow them to watch us as we wrestle with our own questions and the reality that it's not our job to be responsible *for* others, just *to* them. What is our responsibility to them? To share the reason for the hope we have.

> But in your hearts revere Christ as Lord. Always be prepared to give an answer to everyone who asks you to give the reason for the hope that you have. But do this with gentleness and respect (1 Pet. 3:15).

Begin with the End in Mind

When I first started out as a missionary, long before we had children of our own, I hosted missions teams and saw how picky some students were (*I don't eat strawberry jelly; I am sorry, I don't like wheat bread; I only want creamy peanut butter; and so on*). As a result of those experiences, I always switched up my kids PB&J. I never wanted them to complain about their sandwiches at someone else's house. So one week we ate wheat, the next week white. Some days we had strawberry, other days grape. It was a plan. I knew where I wanted to end up, and I was intentional in the process.

It's a silly example, but I think the same principle applies to teaching our children about the Great Commission. If we know where we want them to end up, we should be mindful about the steps in our process. We can introduce them to missional living the same way we teach them to cheer for our college alma mater or to love the beach over the mountains. We can show them the many creative ways to love others well. As a family, what relationships have you invited into your life that are inconvenient? What relationships do you have with families or individuals that don't look, talk or live like you? How do you demonstrate to your family what you value with your discretionary time and money? These questions and many more will propel your family down a path of missional living.

Author and speaker Donald Miller talks about "inciting incidents," in his January 1, 2010, blog entry. He wrote, "*Create an Inciting Incident.* Characters don't want to change. That's why so many New Years resolutions fail. We write down that we want to lose twenty pounds and end up gaining ten. It happens every year. What we are overlooking is a principle that every good screenwriter knows: *Characters don't change without being forced to change.* An inciting incident is the event in a movie that causes upheaval in the protagonist's life. The protagonist, then, naturally seeks to return to stability. And in order to do that, he *HAS* to solve his new problem. . . . Characters must be pressured to change, or they won't. And a narrative context can help. . . . inciting incidents might be signing up with friends for a marathon, joining a kick-boxing class, inviting friends to dinner every Sunday, writing an *I'm Sorry* letter to an old friend, buying an engagement ring, writing a check to a ministry, whatever . . . just something that forces you to move."[1]

Inciting incidents are inviting the neighbor you've been meaning to get to know over to the house for a meal; signing up at church for a Saturday outreach as a family; learning another language; giving away more than a 10 percent offering; following through on any of the million prompts God has given you, and waiting to see what story lies on the other side.

I don't know any better incident inciters than children. They see no boundaries, have little social fear, and believe there is always hope. Listen to the children in your life and then trust alongside of them for how God might be leading.

No Instant Gratification

We want results quickly, don't we? 3G was amazing until we experienced 4G. One drive-through line seemed unbelievable (*food to go in less than 5 minutes?*) until we saw that two lines were more effective. It makes us efficient as a society and allows us to do much more in a day than people a generation ago could, but it can skew our perspective on God's perfect timing. When we help children form relationships, reach out, pray for someone, engage, we need to be helping them to simultaneously understand that God works in ways we can't always see and almost never can measure.

I use a scale with kids to explain that when we first are called into someone's life, he or she might not even know who Jesus is; or worse, may have a negative view of Him. Each interaction, each prayer, hopefully, moves the person along on a path toward salvation. God is the only one who controls the timing of those steps. We are only to be faithful. That means that sometimes we might interact with someone He has been wooing to Himself for a long season, and we get the privilege of witnessing a conversion.

Or, we might talk to someone who not only doesn't understand our faith, but also is hostile toward it. We might not use words in those relationships, just demonstrate consistent love over a long period of time until the questions start to bubble to the surface. Teaching children to trust in God's timing, that results aren't our responsibility, is key to their understanding the Great Commission. Can we say it enough? Our role is obedience and surrender. All else is in the hands of God.

If we can continue to introduce our children to people, not causes, we will awaken the relational nature God stamped into their hearts. We can then listen together as families to the Storyweaver as He writes our next chapters and uses us to share His love with others. It is our high calling and greatest privilege as a parent, teacher or mentor to children. We can model for them and show them they are a part of a tremendously large story. May we all be swept up in this truth.

Remember: A stingy planter gets a stingy crop; a lavish planter gets a lavish crop. I want each of you to take plenty of time to think it over, and make up your own mind what you will give. That will protect you against sob stories and arm-twisting. God loves it when the giver delights in the giving. God can pour on the blessings in astonishing ways so that you're ready for anything and everything, more than just ready to do what needs to be done. *As one psalmist puts it, He throws caution to the winds, giving to the needy in reckless abandon. His right-living, right-giving ways never run out, never wear out.* This most generous God who gives seed to the farmer that becomes bread for your meals is more than extravagant with you. He gives you something you can then give away, which grows into full-formed lives, robust in God, wealthy in every way, so that you can be generous in every way, producing with us great praise to God. Carrying out this social relief work involves far more than helping meet the bare needs of poor Christians. It also produces abundant and bountiful thanksgivings to God. This relief offering is a prod to live at your very best, showing your gratitude to God by being openly obedient to the plain meaning of the Message of Christ. You show your gratitude through your generous offerings to your needy brothers and sisters, and really toward everyone (2 Cor. 9:6-13, *THE MESSAGE*, emphasis added).

DISCUSSION QUESTIONS

1. How are you modeling a missional life for the kids in your ministry?
2. How can we teach kids about what they have to offer?
3. What "burrs" have you heard about under the saddles of the children you serve? What have you done or could you do to cultivate that heart?
4. What do you think it means to give a false sense of accomplishment to children? Give some examples.
5. How or when can you share with children your own Great Commission choices? In what context does that make the most sense?
6. What realities in the world have you tried to keep your children from? How might you be rethinking that now?
7. When you think of inciting incidents, which ones can you point to in your life? How can you encourage children to not be afraid of them?
8. Thinking through instant gratification, what are some biblical examples or real-life stories that can teach this principle of sticking with God's call for the long haul? What are you most afraid of when introducing this kind of lifestyle to children?
9. What do you hear God saying to you right now about missional living?
10. Where do you need to trust God more in this area?

Note

1. Donald Miller, "Living a Good Story, an Alternative to New Years Resolutions," *Storyline*, January 1, 2010. http://storylineblog.com/2010/01/01/living-a-good-story-an-alternative-to-new-years-resolutions/ (accessed October 2013).

Epilogue

RYAN FRANK

Our family has always loved Chicago. We love the Chicago-style hot dogs, walking downtown and being part of the big city, even though it's normally only for a few days at a time. One place we always try to visit when we are in downtown Chicago is the Moody Church. I have a ton of respect for the nineteenth-century evangelist D. L. Moody. I never grow tired of hearing his story.

D. L. Moody's Story

D. L. Moody was born the sixth child of Edwin and Betsy Holton Moody in Northfield, Massachusetts, on February 5, 1837. His formal education ended in the fifth grade, and he rapidly grew tired of life on the farm. He left home at age 17, seeking employment in Boston. Failing to get a job that interested him, he asked his uncle, Samuel Holton, for a job. Reluctantly, Uncle Samuel hired him to work in the retail shoe store he owned. However, to keep young Moody out of trouble, employment was conditional upon his attendance at the Mt. Vernon Congregational Church.

Salvation

At Mt. Vernon, Moody became part of the Sunday School class taught by Edward Kimball. On April 21, 1855, Kimball visited the Holton Shoe Store, found Moody in a stockroom and there spoke to him of the love of Christ. Shortly thereafter, Moody accepted that love and devoted his life to serving God. The following year brought Moody to Chicago with dreams of making his fortune in the shoe business. As success in selling shoes came, so did an interest in providing Sunday School classes for Chicago's children and the local YMCA.

YMCA

During the revival of 1857 to 1858, Moody became more involved with the YMCA, performing janitorial jobs for the organization and serving wherever they needed him. In 1860, when he left the business world, he began spending more and more time serving the organization. In fact, in the 1861 to 1862 annual report, Moody was praised for all of his efforts. Although they could not pay him, the YMCA recommended he stay "employed" as city missionary.

Mission Sunday School

Meanwhile, Moody's Mission Sunday School flourished. What set this ministry apart was Moody's desire to reach the "lost" youth of the city, the children with little to no education, less than ideal family situations, and poor economic circumstances. Soon the Sunday School outgrew the converted saloon used as a meeting hall. As the classes grew, associates encouraged Moody to begin his own church. Eventually, on February 28, 1864, the Illinois Street Church (now The Moody Church) opened in its own building with Moody as pastor.

Civil War

As the political landscape of the United States changed in the 1860s, Moody's connection with the YMCA proved a useful tool in his ministry. As the Civil War approached, the Union Army mobilized volunteer soldiers across the north. Camp Douglas was established outside of Chicago, which Moody saw as a great evangelistic opportunity. Along with a few others, Moody created the Committee on Devotional Meetings to minister to the troops stationed at Camp Douglas, the 72nd Illinois Volunteer Regiment. This was just the beginning of Moody's Civil War outreach. From 1861 to 1865, he ministered on battlefields and throughout the city, state and country to thousands of soldiers, both Union and Confederate. All the while, he maintained the Mission Sunday School.

Training School for Women

While ministering in Chicago, Moody and his wife met a woman named Emma Dryer, a successful teacher and administrator. Moody was impressed with her zeal for ministry and her educational background. He knew that women had a unique ability to evangelize mothers and children in a way that men never could, and saw Dryer as just the person to help him encourage this group.

Moody asked Dryer to oversee a ministry specifically to train women for evangelistic outreach and missionary work. Under Dryer's leadership, the training program grew rapidly, and so did her desire for this ministry to reach men as well as women. She continued to pray that the Lord would place the idea for such a school on Moody's heart.

The Chicago Fire

On Sunday, October 8, 1871, as Moody came to the end of his sermon for the evening, the city fire bell began to ring. At first, no one thought much about it, as these city bells often rung. However, this night was different—it was the beginning of the Great Chicago Fire. Moody's first concern was for his family, locating them and making sure they were somewhere safe. After securing his family's safety, Moody and his wife stayed in the north side of the city to help other residents. The fire finally burned out Tuesday afternoon, after consuming much of what Moody had built.

This was a poignant time in Moody's life and the fire forced him to re-evaluate his ministry. It was during this time of evaluation that he realized he needed to heed the Lord's call on his life. For years, he had been moving forward and then asking God to support his plans. He knew from this point on, his call was to preach the Word of God to the world.

Revival Abroad

In June 1872, Moody made his first trip to the United Kingdom, during which a few close contacts urged him to come back in a year. In June 1873, Moody, his wife, Emma, their children, good friend and musician Ira Sankey, and his wife, all traveled from New York to Liverpool, England. Moody and Sankey traveled throughout the UK and Ireland, holding meetings and helping to fuel the revival that was slowly sweeping the region. Moody's visit made a lasting impression, inspiring lay people across the region to begin children's ministries and ministry training schools for women.

Moody was revolutionary in his evangelistic approach. Despite conflicting counsel from friends and trusted contacts, he and Sankey traveled to Ireland during a time when Catholics and Protestants were constantly at odds with each other. Moody was different: He did not care what denomination a person claimed; he just wanted the message of Christ to be heard. As a result, the revival swept into Ireland, and he won praises from both Catholics and Protestants.

1875–1878

After two years overseas, the Moody family finally returned to the United States. They settled in Northfield, where Moody was born and raised, and he began to plan his next round of evangelistic city campaigns. From October 1875 to May 1876, Moody and three other evangelists toured through the major cities of the Midwest and Atlantic coast, preaching the message of salvation. Moody would embark on yet another city campaign before his desire to train young Christian workers would grip him again.

Moody's Schools

Moody was on the cutting edge of ministry, and in 1879, Moody opened the Northfield Seminary for Young Women to provide young women the opportunity to gain an education. Not long after, Moody created the Mount Hermon School for Boys with the same goal as the girls' school—to educate the poor and minorities. Moody had an amazing ability to bridge the gap between denominations, which was apparent in the diverse religious backgrounds of the school's students.

In 1886, Emma Dryer's prayers were answered and the Chicago Evangelization Society (today, Moody Bible Institute) was founded. Moody had been focused on ministry near his home in Northfield, but he came out to Chicago to help raise money for the Society, to support Dryer, and to see his dream become a reality. The Chicago Evangelization Society had been Moody's vision but really came to fruition because of Dryer's hard work.

That same year, Moody assembled a large group of college students at Mount Hermon for the first "College Students' Summer School." This conference would birth the Student Volunteer Movement for Foreign Missions. By 1911, it was estimated that 5,000 student volunteers from America alone had come out of the program. Moody's vision for the mission movement grew as it spread around the world to Europe and South Africa.

Later Years

Moody continued to evangelize throughout America, often preaching in major cities and at various universities. His heart was for his schools, and he spent much of his time in Northfield. Moody was a visionary who always seemed a step ahead of the status quo. From training women to reaching out to lost children to bridging the gap between denominations, he was unlike any other.

Moody was a man of great discernment. He had an innate ability to find capable, godly people to put into positions of leadership and bring his ideas to fruition. This enabled him to continue his evangelistic outreach while his ministries flourished. Throughout his life, Moody always found time to be with his family, making every effort to show his love and care for them.

Moody died December 22, 1899, surrounded by his family.

What a life! Every time I read his story I am moved to dream bigger and do more. Here's the amazing thing that I left out of the story. Toward the end of Moody's life, he said this: "If I could relive my life, I would devote my entire ministry to reaching children for God." Wow! Let that settle in. If he could do it all over again, he would focus *all* of his ministry on children.

Serving in children's ministry is a blessing. It is also a calling that we should each take seriously. My friend Roger Fields, who wrote chapter 13 of this book, wrote a declaration titled, "The Calling." I'll close the book with his words. May they bless your heart and be your prayer.

The Calling

I am a minister. I minister to the largest mission field in the world. I minister to children.

My calling is sure. My challenge is big. My vision is clear. My desire is strong. My influence is eternal. My impact is critical. My values are solid. My faith is tough. My mission is urgent. My purpose is unmistakable. My direction is forward. My heart is genuine. My strength is supernatural. My reward is promised. And my God is real.

In a world of cynicism, I offer hope. In a world of confusion, I offer truth. In a world of immorality, I offer values. In a world of neglect, I offer attention. In a world of abuse, I offer safety. In a world of ridicule, I offer affirmation. In a world of division, I offer reconciliation. In a world of bitterness, I offer forgiveness. In a world of sin, I offer salvation. In a world of hate, I offer God's love.

I refuse to be dismayed, disengaged, disgruntled, discouraged or distracted. Neither will I look back, stand back, fall back, go back or sit back. I do not need applause, flattery, adulation, prestige, stature or veneration. I do not have time for business as usual, mediocre standards, small thinking, outdated methods, normal expectations, average results, ordinary ideas, petty disputes or low vision. I will not give up, give in, bail out, lie down, turn over, quit or surrender.

I will pray when things look bad. I will pray when things look good. I will move forward when others stand still. I will trust God when obstacles arise. I will work when the task is overwhelming. I will get up when I fall down.

My calling is to reach boys and girls for God. It is too serious to be taken lightly, too urgent to be postponed, too vital to be ignored, too relevant to be overlooked, too significant to be trivialized, too eternal to be fleeting and too passionate to be quenched.

I know my mission. I know my challenge. I also know my limitations, my weaknesses, my fears and my problems. And I know my God. Let others get the praise. Let the church get the blessing. Let God get the glory.

I am a minister. I minister to children. This is who I am. This is what I do.[1]

Note

1. Roger Fields, "The Callling," *Kidz Blitz Live.* http://kidzblitz.com/the-calling/(accessed October 2013).

Meet the new KidzMatter.com!

Updated daily and featuring only the freshest stories, ideas, resources, and more. Plus, you'll love this thriving community of children's ministry leaders and bloggers. The brand new KidzMatter.com is your hub for all things Kidmin.

Check it out today.

KidzMatter.com